Educating Newcomers

K–12 Public Schooling for Undocumented and Asylum-Seeking Children in the United States

SHELLY CULBERTSON, JULIA H. KAUFMAN, JENNA W. KRAMER,
BRIAN PHILLIPS

RAND EDUCATION AND LABOR

For more information on this publication, visit **www.rand.org/t/RRA1326-1**.

About RAND

The RAND Corporation is a research organization that develops solutions to public policy challenges to help make communities throughout the world safer and more secure, healthier and more prosperous. RAND is nonprofit, nonpartisan, and committed to the public interest. To learn more about RAND, visit www.rand.org.

Research Integrity

Our mission to help improve policy and decisionmaking through research and analysis is enabled through our core values of quality and objectivity and our unwavering commitment to the highest level of integrity and ethical behavior. To help ensure our research and analysis are rigorous, objective, and nonpartisan, we subject our research publications to a robust and exacting quality-assurance process; avoid both the appearance and reality of financial and other conflicts of interest through staff training, project screening, and a policy of mandatory disclosure; and pursue transparency in our research engagements through our commitment to the open publication of our research findings and recommendations, disclosure of the source of funding of published research, and policies to ensure intellectual independence. For more information, visit www.rand.org/about/principles.

RAND's publications do not necessarily reflect the opinions of its research clients and sponsors.

Published by the RAND Corporation, Santa Monica, Calif.
© 2021 RAND Corporation
RAND® is a registered trademark.

Library of Congress Cataloging-in-Publication Data is available for this publication.
ISBN: 978-1-9774-0740-5

Cover image: andresr/Getty Images.

About This Report

Migration over the U.S. southwest border in the past decade has been composed of growing numbers of undocumented and asylum-seeking families and children from Mexico and Central America, with particular increases in numbers starting in fiscal year (FY) 2017. By U.S. law, states must provide education to all children, regardless of immigration status. Yet sufficient information needed for policymaking is lacking, in particular about the ages and geographic locations of the children by state and district, needs for teachers and staff to accommodate these children, and experiences and good practices in schools. This report models the numbers of such children by state between FYs 2017 and 2019, reviews the federal policy landscape for their education, and provides case studies of how schools are managing education for them in Jefferson Parish Schools in Louisiana and Oakland Unified School District in California.

This report specifically aims to help various stakeholders understand the broad range of issues and implications related to large influxes in undocumented and asylum-seeking children over the southwest border, including the affordances and challenges of current federal and state immigration policies, numbers of school staff necessary to serve these students, and critical strategies and remaining challenges for supporting these children in U.S. school systems. Drawing on our research, we offer recommendations to school leaders, state officials, and federal policymakers about how to better provide education for this population and support schools in doing so. This report will be of interest to policymakers engaged in issues of migration, school districts with large or growing immigrant populations, state education officials around the United States, federal policymakers, and academics interested in these topics.

RAND Education and Labor

This study was undertaken by RAND Education and Labor, a division of the RAND Corporation that conducts research on early childhood through postsecondary education programs, workforce development, and programs and policies affecting workers, entrepreneurship, and financial literacy and decisionmaking.

More information about RAND can be found at www.rand.org. Questions about this report should be directed to Shelly Culbertson (shellyc@rand.org), and questions about RAND Education and Labor should be directed to educationandlabor@rand.org.

Funding

Funding for this research was provided by gifts from RAND supporters and income from operations.

Acknowledgments

The authors would like to acknowledge the following people for their contributions to this work. First, at the RAND Corporation, thank you to Gabriella Gonzalez and Michael Pollard, who advised and made considerable contributions to the analysis for this work, and to Paige Rudin for her contributions in data collection and the literature review. This document benefited substantively from quality assurance feedback from Fatih Unlu and Katherine Carman, publications management from Monette Velasco, and expert editing from Rebecca Fowler. Thank you to Kristin Leuschner for her excellent communications work on this report, as well as to Stephanie Lonsinger for helping to prepare this report for publication. Second, thanks to our interviewees, including the policy officials, educators, and others who took time to talk with us. In particular, we would like to thank the wonderful administrators and staff at Jefferson Parish Schools and the Oakland Unified School District. This work would not be possible without your valuable insights. Third, we would like to thank the reviewers of this report—Margarita Pivovarova (assistant professor of education economics at the Mary Lou Fulton Teachers College at Arizona State University), Renae Skarin (senior director of content at the English Learners Success Forum), and Margaret Weden (acting director of the Population Research Center at RAND)—for their helpful input, which made this report much stronger. Any flaws that remain are solely the authors' responsibility.

Summary

Undocumented and asylum-seeking immigrant populations have been crossing the U.S. southwest border at increasing rates, with a surge from fiscal years (FYs) 2017 through 2019. Although migration flows slowed in FY 2020 during the COVID-19 pandemic, FY 2021 is on pace for the biggest migration surge there in two decades (Chiacu, 2021). This has included increasing numbers of families and unaccompanied children, with most coming from the Northern Triangle countries of Honduras, Guatemala, and El Salvador, as well as Mexico. There are multiple overlapping factors that have contributed to the migration of children across the southwest U.S. border, including high levels of gang violence and intimidation in Northern Triangle countries, poverty and lack of economic opportunity, natural disasters, poor governance, and U.S. asylum procedures that benefit minors and therefore incentivize migration.

Although multiple aspects of immigration policy are subject to debate, and the federal government has taken steps to reduce the flow of undocumented and asylum-seeking immigrants at the border (Pérez and Hackman, 2021), less attention has been paid to what happens after children are inside the United States. One area of ongoing importance to U.S. federal, state, and local policymakers is how to address the critical policy issues accompanying surges in migration and the growing number of families and children involved, including the demands placed on public services and options for meeting the needs of immigrants and their host communities. In particular, the migration of undocumented and asylum-seeking children across the border has a considerable impact on K–12 public schools, which are federally required to serve and support these students, many of whom have little formal education, are English-language learners (ELLs), are in impoverished households, and have symptoms of psychological distress and trauma (Camarota, Griffith, and Zeigler, 2017). Yet sufficient information needed for policymaking is lacking, in particular about the ages and geographic locations of the children by state and district, needs for teachers and staff to accommodate them, and experiences and good practices in schools.

The goal of this report is to understand how states and local communities manage K–12 public education for undocumented and asylum-seeking children (typically children under age 18 upon arrival), taking into account various aspects of these children's experiences. It specifically aims to help various stakeholders understand the range of issues related to supporting these newcomer children and the schools that educate them. Our research addresses the following questions:

- How many recently arrived (from FYs 2017 through 2019) undocumented and asylum-seeking children from Mexico and Central America are in the United States, where are they, and what factors affect how many more of these children might arrive over the next several years?

- What are the federal and state policy landscapes for the education of undocumented and asylum-seeking children?
- What approaches are school systems taking for these children's education?
- How can state and local education systems be prepared and supported to educate these children?

We explore these questions through a rich mix of quantitative and qualitative research, including (1) models of the numbers and locations of undocumented and asylum-seeking children who have crossed the southwest border from FYs 2017 through 2019 and enrolled in schools, along with implications for new teacher and staff needs; (2) federal and state policy analysis and interviews with officials from federal and state governments and other policy organizations; and (3) interviews and focus groups with administrators and educators who are tasked with supporting all immigrant children—including those who may be undocumented or asylum seeking—in two case study K–12 school districts.

The Number and Locations of Undocumented and Asylum-Seeking Children from the Northern Triangle and Mexico

We estimate that about 575,000 children from the Northern Triangle and Mexico encountered U.S. Customs and Border Protection (CBP) officials at the southwest border over the FYs 2017–2019 period. About 491,000 of these children remained in the country in unre-

A Note on the Population of Children Included in This Study

In this report, we use the phrase *undocumented and asylum-seeking children* to describe the population of children considered.

The populations in this study consist of both those who crossed the border without valid U.S. immigration or visa documentation and were detained by CBP (referred to as *apprehensions*) and those who arrived at the border and turned themselves in to CBP to claim asylum (referred to as *inadmissibles*, although many are admitted to the United States while they wait for their asylum case to be processed). CBP cites numbers of children found at the border in both of these categories as *encounters*.

These children are both those who arrived in the United States unaccompanied and those who arrived as part of a family group. There are many similarities between children who arrived with families and those who arrived unaccompanied, and in much of the analysis of this report, we treat them as the same group. Yet there are key differences as well, which we note throughout. For instance, children who arrived unaccompanied and who are placed with other relatives or new families as sponsors might face additional challenges in adapting to new home lives than those who arrived with families.

solved status as of March 2020, and about 321,000 of them were enrolled in K–12 schools at that time. Most children arriving in family units (77 percent) were age 12 or younger, while most unaccompanied children (74 percent) were teenagers ages 15 to 17.

Some states and counties are experiencing larger impacts from these recent arrivals than others, although it is likely that impacts are more locally concentrated than we could identify in the data. California, Texas, Florida, New York, Virginia, Maryland, New Jersey, Georgia, North Carolina, and Louisiana together account for about 75 percent of the recent arrivals. Each of these ten states is home to more that 10,000 recent arrivals except Louisiana (home to an estimated 9,200), as illustrated in Figure S.1. As of March 2020, new undocumented and asylum-seeking arrivals as a share of baseline K–12 student enrollment (i.e., in the 2016–2017 school year) reached 1 percent in five of these ten states: Maryland (1.9 percent), Virginia (1.4 percent), Louisiana (1.3 percent), Florida (1.1 percent), and New Jersey (1.0 percent).

To support these recent arrivals without changing teacher-student and staff-student ratios, school systems in seven states would each have needed to hire at least 1,000 additional teachers and at least 1,000 additional other teaching and administrative staff, if enrollment was otherwise unchanged. In particular, schools in Los Angeles County, California, and Harris County, Texas (which includes Houston), alone would need at least an additional 1,000 teachers to maintain their baseline teacher-student ratios.

FIGURE S.1

Estimated Distribution Across States of Recently Arrived Undocumented and Asylum-Seeking Children from Mexico and the Northern Triangle in Primary- and Secondary-School Systems, as of March 2020

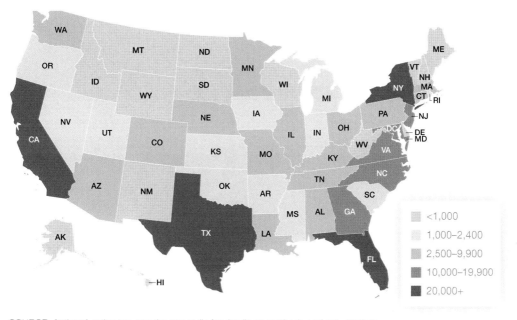

SOURCE: Authors' estimates; see the appendix for details on methods and assumptions.

The recent arrivals add to baseline numbers of students in schools who are Hispanic and likely also add to the numbers who have limited English proficiency or are ELLs or are eligible for or receive free or reduced-price lunches. These arrivals represent more than 5 percent of the baseline Hispanic student population in nine states and the District of Columbia, as shown in Figure S.2. These states include Louisiana (where the arrivals are 20 percent of baseline Hispanic students), Maryland, Virginia, and Georgia—also among the top ten states in the number of recent arrivals. The others—Tennessee, Kentucky, Missouri, Mississippi, Nebraska, and the District of Columbia—are experiencing among the largest impacts relative to the baseline population of Hispanic students but are not among the states with the largest impacts in terms of overall numbers of students. These two pieces of information—numbers and relative shares—provide complementary information about where impacts on schools are concentrated.

Since FY 2019, the last year of arrivals we consider in our estimates, the COVID-19 pandemic resulted in substantial decreases in the flow of children to the southwest border, likely due to both more-strict policies keeping any new immigrants from entering the United States and less migration because of the pandemic itself. Border encounters with children and family units fell precipitously at the outset of the pandemic in 2020, then rebounded in early 2021.

FIGURE S.2

Estimated Distribution Across States of Recently Arrived Undocumented and Asylum-Seeking Children from Mexico and the Northern Triangle as a Share of the Baseline Hispanic Population in Primary- and Secondary-School Systems, as of March 2020

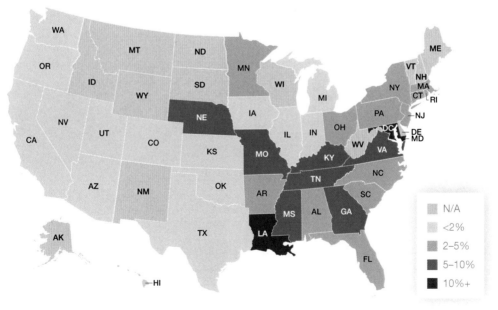

SOURCE: Authors' estimates; see the appendix for details on methods and assumptions.
NOTE: *N/A* (not available) indicates the inability to reliably estimate a percentage because there are fewer than 1,000 children.

Meanwhile, Title 42, a Trump administration–era public health policy that has continued with modifications under the Biden administration, has been used to turn back migrants on public health grounds, including children who might otherwise have been admitted into the country to pursue asylum. In tandem, these factors suggest that the number of recent arrivals entering the country and ultimately K–12 schools fell throughout much of 2020.

The Federal and State Policy Landscapes

Federal Policy Regarding Education

Undocumented and asylum-seeking children entering the United States encounter a complex policy ecosystem that shapes their transition to American life and educational experience. The box below briefly summarizes the key federal policies relevant to the population in our study. Federal law guarantees the right to an education for all minor children in the United States, which was codified in the Bill of Rights and reaffirmed in Titles IV and VI of the Civil Rights Act of 1964. Supreme Court rulings have established that children have a right to education regardless of immigration status (*Plyler v. Doe*, 1982), set requirements regarding the provision of education while in federal custody (*Reno v. Flores*, 1997), and clarified constitutional educational practices for children with limited English proficiency (*Lau v. Nichols*, 1974).

Key Policies Supporting Access to Education for Newcomer Immigrant Children and Youth

- U.S. Bill of Rights and Civil Rights Act of 1964: All children in the United States are guaranteed equal access to educational opportunity, regardless of citizenship and immigration status.
- *Lau v. Nichols* (1974): This Supreme Court ruling requires equal treatment for non–English-speaking students and ruled that districts must make affirmative remedial efforts to ensure a "meaningful education" for all regardless of language background (e.g., through the provision of supplemental language instruction).
- Lau Remedies (1975): The U.S. Department of Health, Education, and Welfare issued a set of pedagogical guidelines for schools to promote the provision of an equal education for non–English-speaking students.
- *Plyler v. Doe* (1982): This Supreme Court ruling reaffirmed that school-age children are entitled to education, regardless of the immigration status of their parents.
- *Reno v. Flores* (1997): This Supreme Court ruling found that unaccompanied children cannot be detained by CBP for longer than 20 days, which has educational implications, given that CBP does not provide educational supports.

State Policy Regarding Education

State policies related to immigration and education shape undocumented and asylum-seeking children's access to public education, as well as the quality of that education. State policy regarding undocumented and asylum-seeking individuals can affect the educational experiences of such children living in those states by shaping their interactions with public organizations—specifically, K–12 schools. State laws related particularly to the education of immigrant children and children with limited English often are related to the provision of enhanced learning opportunities for refugees or ELLs in K–12 education or immigration and residency requirements for access to in-state tuition or financial assistance at colleges and universities (Morse et al., 2016). States have taken different approaches to legislation and policies regarding immigration and enforcement, K–12 educational pedagogy and resources, and access to in-state tuition and state financial assistance for postsecondary education, all of which contribute to the complex policy context for the education of these children.

Federal and State Responsibilities and Impediments Regarding the Education of Undocumented and Asylum-Seeking Children

Federal Resources and Responsibilities

Federal programs administered by the U.S. Department of Education (through state and local education agencies) are intended to provide resources to local education agencies to support newcomers' development of English proficiency and mitigate the negative academic impacts of educational disruption, regardless of their immigration status. The U.S. Department of Education provides two major resources for the education of children: It administers formula grant programs, and it develops materials and convenes professionals to support states and districts in meeting federal requirements for educational provision. The 2015 Every Student Succeeds Act (ESSA) authorizes more than $24.5 billion in funding to be distributed across multiple programs. The formula grant programs of note for the support of the education of this population of children are the Title I (Parts A and C) and Title III programs established by the 1965 Elementary and Secondary Education Act (ESEA): Title I funds programs intended to promote access to quality education for disadvantaged students; it indirectly supports undocumented and asylum-seeking children by providing school funding (through Part A) intended to address disadvantages across a range of immigrant populations. Title III directly supports quality education and language instruction by developing and sustaining programs related to English proficiency, professional development for school staff, and activities to promote community engagement (Thornley, 2017). The U.S. Department of Education also produces guidance materials and connects professionals to assist school administrators in navigating the complex federal policy landscape and seeks to build the capacity of state education agencies (SEAs) by connecting staff within a program.

Obstacles to Local Education Agencies Receiving Available Federal Support

According to our interviews with stakeholders, the chief impediments to federal support for undocumented and asylum-seeking children were understanding of the law, navigation of the policy context, and receipt of adequate funding. Stakeholders pointed to gaps in understanding what is federally required of states and local education agencies. The complex policy ecosystem surrounding the legal status and educational experience of undocumented and asylum-seeking children is a key impediment. Although federal law guarantees minors' right to an education, and U.S. Department of Education grantmaking programs are intended to ensure that states and districts have adequate resources to serve these students, the laws and programs often breed misunderstanding for students, families, and educational staff alike; policies also leave gaps in support of students' needs beyond their academic enrichment. Stakeholders also expressed concern regarding the flow of financial resources intended for the education of this population, with some congressional staff noting that allocated funds targeted for the support of education and services for undocumented and asylum-seeking children are sometimes diverted to shore up funding to support general programs and expenses for all children.

State Resources and Responsibilities

SEAs are responsible for administering federal and state education laws, dispersing federal and state financial resources, and providing guidance and support for local education agencies or school districts. SEAs are expected to monitor district adherence to the federal requirement that undocumented and asylum-seeking children have a right to an education, ensure that districts obey state education law regarding student eligibility for enrollment and instructional practices, collect data and create systems for holding districts accountable for the academic progress their students make, and license and verify the qualification of teachers. SEAs also play a key role in facilitating access to and administration of federal grant programs, which flow through or are administered by SEAs, which make and monitor subgrants to local education agencies. SEAs collect data from local education agencies regarding their student population and student progress, analyze these data, and report up to the U.S. Department of Education, leveraging this information to identify needs and justify federal grant applications. SEAs also provide guidance for districts, develop and distribute informational materials on complex policy areas or problems of practice, and provide training for district staff.

Key Differences in How States Support Undocumented and Asylum-Seeking Children

There is variation from state to state in the laws that shape the experiences of undocumented and asylum-seeking children. First, the minimum and maximum school enrollment ages vary by state, which can have ramifications for whether and what type of educational opportunities are offered to undocumented and asylum-seeking children. Second, eligibility for public benefits varies by state, and—in states with fewer benefits—undocumented and asylum-seeking teenagers may feel compelled to drop out of school and work, and families may face considerable challenges to ensuring that their children regularly attend school. Third, in most states, undocumented and asylum-seeking children are not eligible for in-state college and university tuition and state financial aid (Morse, 2021; Serna, Cohen, and Nguyen, 2017), and undocumented children are not eligible for federal financial aid, so state tuition policies and aid eligibility are important factors that shape the accessibility of postsecondary training for these children. Fourth, the local labor market, opportunities for further training, and the degree of stringency or leniency regarding certification and licensure all have implications for the staffing and quality of educational instruction for undocumented and asylum-seeking children. In addition, differences in policy and practice at the local level—such as varying requirements for proof of residency—contribute to differences in the educational experiences of these children, and front-line district staff in districts sometimes create undue administrative burden for children and families through unwitting or willful complication of enrollment and ongoing administrative processes.

Educator Experiences in California and Louisiana

We conducted two case studies, which focused on school experiences with undocumented and asylum-seeking students in two very different contexts: Jefferson Parish Schools in Louisiana and Oakland Unified School District in California. We selected these case studies to include one district that experienced large, recent increases in the population of children in this study (Jefferson Parish) and include a second district that has been serving large numbers of these children for many years (Oakland Unified). Both are in the top ten states and top 40 districts nationally in terms of numbers of newly arriving students. One is in a sanctuary state (i.e., a state whose laws limit the extent to which state and local law enforcement can collaborate with federal agencies on deportation) (California), and one is not (Louisiana). We examined the challenges faced by districts and useful approaches for supporting these children, as summarized in Table S.1. Readers should keep in mind that the challenges and approaches we identified are necessarily limited by the numbers and range of interviewees with whom we were able to speak, as well as the limitations of focusing on only two school districts among the over 13,000 school districts across the United States. In addition, our case study informants sometimes spoke of the practices and supports for all immigrant students (the vast majority of whom are from Central America or Mexico), since they do not necessarily have knowledge of which students are undocumented or asylum seeking. Nonetheless, our case study informants provided us with some useful insights for policy and practice.

The challenges that undocumented and asylum-seeking students face are considerable and wide ranging. Both districts found that documentation requirements and online enrollment could hinder access to school for children of parents who speak little English, may be transient or struggle to produce required residency documentation, and have low computer literacy and access. Staff in both districts noted language barriers as an obstacle to

TABLE S.1

Summary of Challenges and Useful Approaches Taken by Case Study Districts

Category	Challenges	Useful Approaches
Enrollment	• Language barriers for both parents and children, including barriers related to appropriate language testing and placement • Documentation requirements	• Guaranteed in-person enrollment with language supports for students and families • Simplified intake processes • Students referred to nonacademic services at the time of enrollment
English-language learning and academics	• Language barriers for children and teachers, including lack of bilingual staff for all languages spoken by children and large variation in English-language skills of incoming students • Difficulty in determining how and when to integrate newcomer ELLs into regular classrooms with students who speak English proficiently • Lack of good instructional materials and approaches for students who come to school far below their age-appropriate grade level, called *students with interrupted formal education* • Not enough support for undocumented students to pursue careers after high school	• Specific programs and supports for newcomer students • Treating language skills as an asset, including dual-language programs • Supportive high school models
Nonacademic supports	• The trauma and culture shock that many undocumented and asylum-seeking students are experiencing or have experienced • The poverty and lack of access to basic necessities among many students and their families • Weak family support at home for many students • Students' legal needs • Low attendance, truancy, and dropouts	• Approaches to build community and trust among students and families, as well as celebrate their diverse backgrounds and culture • Specialized staff to meet students' social and emotional needs • Referrals and partnerships with other community programs • Trauma-informed instruction that takes into account the challenges students have faced and their resilience to move beyond these challenges
Teacher training	• Need for with expertise in language learning in Jefferson Parish • Need for specialized credentials to support approaches for dual languages and students with interrupted formal education	• Specialized staff who push in to support teachers • Intensive professional learning opportunities

enrollment, as well as academics, and described the challenge of determining when to integrate newcomer ELLs into regular classrooms with students who speak English proficiently. Another challenge to academics was the lack of sufficient-quality instructional materials and approaches for students who may come to school far below their age-appropriate grade level.

Staff also reported challenges in helping students consider postsecondary education and career options.

Immigration status exacerbates all those challenges because policies limit the extent to which undocumented and asylum-seeking children are eligible for benefits, such as health insurance and postsecondary financial support, as well as because undocumented and asylum-seeking children and families may be distracted by legal considerations and financial needs. District staff described a range of nonacademic challenges that undocumented and asylum-seeking students face, including issues related to trauma and culture shock, lack of access to basic necessities, weak family support at home, legal issues, and absenteeism among students.

Staff in both districts described the need for more teacher training for serving all ELLs, including those who may be undocumented or asylum seeking. Jefferson Parish administrators focused on the need for more bilingual teachers and teachers trained to support English learning, while Oakland Unified administrators focused on ensuring that teachers have the more-specialized credentials needed to support dual-language approaches and to support students with interrupted formal education.

Both districts provide all ELLs—and particularly those who may be undocumented or asylum seeking—with numerous resources and supports and address the challenges described here through multiple approaches.

To support enrollment in school, districts use in-person enrollment approaches, simplify intake processes, and provide referrals to nonacademic services. To support academic achievement among this population, both districts have developed thoughtful approaches to providing ELLs with support specific to their newcomer needs, such as dual-language approaches, some initial period (one year in Jefferson Parish, three years in Oakland Unified) when they can focus on newcomer education without being overwhelmed by being in classes with their English-speaking peers, and assistant teacher *paraprofessionals* who support ELLs in regular classrooms. Each district has specialized staff who *push in* and provide support to ELLs within teachers' classrooms as they are teaching all students (as opposed to *pulling* ELLs out of the classroom for specialized instruction apart from their peers). In Jefferson Parish, for example, teachers and administrators noted that English-as-a-second-language (ESL) coaches provide training, professional development, and feedback for regular classroom teachers with ELLs. In addition, each district has established intensive professional learning opportunities, although those opportunities are sometimes expensive and difficult to offer consistently.

School districts have also put numerous supports in place to address students' nonacademic needs, including efforts to improve trust between district staff, students, and families; partnerships with community services; and various social and emotional supports. Both districts have specialized staff to support students' nonacademic needs, including social and emotional wellbeing, and both maintain a network of outside resources to which they can refer students. In Oakland Unified, staff spoke frequently about the need to provide "trauma-informed instruction" that supports students' social and emotional needs.

At the same time, these districts acknowledge that available resources do not necessarily meet the full needs of these students, particularly those who might not have family support at home and those who have come into the district with gaps in their formal education. Funding and accountability policies may create obstacles to providing those supports. Because California provides some services to all children—such as health insurance and access to higher education—regardless of their immigration status, Oakland Unified links school enrollment with other supports. Yet those policies may also place larger burdens on school systems to ensure that students are taking advantage of those services, even though state and federal funding for schools does not include financial assistance to support these efforts.

Recommendations

Although school districts have made many efforts to address the education needs of undocumented and asylum-seeking children, the growing numbers of such children arriving and the diverse needs of this population have increased the pressure on schools. We developed a series of recommendations for federal and state policymakers, as well as school districts, which we summarize here.

Develop Policies and Processes to Address the Initial Needs of Undocumented and Asylum-Seeking Children When They Cross the Border

- **Develop and improve definitions, data, and information sources.** Data about the numbers, locations, and ages of undocumented and asylum-seeking children are not available to the extent needed to support national policymaking. We recommend improving mechanisms for tracking these children and analyzing their performance without collecting sensitive information or endangering children and families, including creating goals and outcome measures.
- **Create agreements for educational records transfers with Northern Triangle countries.** Although the United States has a memorandum of understanding with Mexico for educational record transfers for students from Mexico enrolling in U.S. schools, it does not have similar agreements with Guatemala, Honduras, and El Salvador, but there are growing numbers of students from these countries in U.S. schools. Educational records are important for establishing grade-level equivalency and students' educational needs.
- **Create opportunities for collaboration and discussion among the Office of Refugee Resettlement, community services, and local education agencies.** Many undocumented and asylum-seeking children fall through the cracks at the point when they are released from the Office of Refugee Resettlement to a sponsor; then the responsibility for their education shifts to local education agencies and their sponsors. We therefore recommend that the office—possibly along with other federal and state agencies—consider

collaborating more closely with community service providers and local departments of health, including those who might provide more-robust social services, medical services, and legal supports than schools are able to provide.

Develop Policies and Processes to Address the Needs of Undocumented and Asylum-Seeking Children When They Are in K–12 Schools

- **Provide additional funding for schools with immigration surges on a rolling basis.** New students in this population arrive at schools throughout the year, yet schools must request funding based on student populations in August of each year, which might not align with when students arrive and which can leave schools stretched financially when they experience midyear surges in enrollment of immigrant children. We recommend that schools have the option to request federal funding more frequently than annually, as populations change, such as quarterly.
- **Increase funding and resources for nonacademic supports for students.** Newly arriving undocumented and asylum-seeking children often enter U.S. schools grappling with substantial trauma from their lives in their countries of origin or their journeys to the United States, and school districts may have limited resources to address students' mental health needs. The provision of federal and state resources to support the hiring and professional development of mental health and counseling services would expand access to much-needed counseling supports.
- **Strategically develop, recruit, and place professionals with relevant language and other needed skills in school districts.** School districts are facing a shortage of education professionals who have the language skills and appropriate certifications to support newcomers. Creating provisions for emergency waivers or certification opportunities will expand the labor markets from which districts can recruit staff. It would also be beneficial to expand opportunities to undertake needed training and earn certifications. Jefferson Parish Schools particularly viewed its paraprofessional model to help ELLs in regular classrooms as effective, and this approach could be tried elsewhere.
- **Provide professional learning and high-quality resources to all teachers to support ELLs.** Our research suggests that most school systems across the United States have enrolled at least some undocumented and asylum-seeking children. Thus, we recommend that all teachers across the United States receive at least some training to support the language, other academic, social, and emotional growth of these students. One of the largest challenges the educators spoke about with us is that of supporting students with interrupted formal education. The challenges faced by these students point to the need for many more opportunities for collaboration among schools and educators that serve this population, as well as repositories and one-stop shops for materials and train-

ing to support these populations. This should also include more readily available assessments in Spanish to help schools with grade placement for such incoming students.

- **Provide information and training for all school staff who engage with newly arriving children.** All school system staff—including administrators, any instructional staff, and noninstructional staff, from school secretaries to perhaps even bus drivers—should possess a thorough and up-to-date understanding of the responsibilities of the school and district to enroll and provide a quality education for newly arriving children, as well as the immigration policies that may affect children's school experiences.

- **Create more-targeted career and technical education approaches.** A key challenge in both case study school districts was in preparing high school ELL students who were academically behind for the workforce after high school. Challenges included lacking targeted skills programs relevant to the types of jobs available in the labor market and the need to integrate English-language, relevant math, and technical skills into single courses; requirements for social security numbers for minors to take certain certification tests; and the lack of high school graduation pathways for students with interrupted formal education. The U.S. Department of Education and SEAs should develop federal or state guidance regarding secondary training opportunities.

- **Improve the evidence base about critical underresearched areas.** There are multiple areas in which the evidence base should be improved to support the education of undocumented and asylum-seeking children, such as those related to data, educational approaches, community relations, cross-state comparisons, and teacher training.

Contents

Figures and Tables

Figures

Tables

CHAPTER ONE

Introduction

Undocumented and asylum-seeking immigrant populations crossing the U.S. southwest border have been surging. Indeed, there was a particular surge from fiscal years (FYs) 2017 through 2019. Although migration slowed in 2020 during the COVID-19 pandemic, at the time this report was being written, 2021 was on pace to be the year with the biggest migration surge at the U.S. southwest border in two decades (Chiacu, 2021). In the past, most such migration involved single adults from Mexico seeking economic opportunities. However, recent migration has included increasing numbers of families and unaccompanied children, both from Mexico and from the Northern Triangle countries of Honduras, Guatemala, and El Salvador. These migrants are people seeking better economic opportunities and those fleeing gang violence and problems with the rule of law.

Although the U.S. government has taken steps to reduce the flow of undocumented and asylum-seeking immigrants at the border (Pérez and Hackman, 2021), less attention has been paid to what happens after such newly arriving children are inside the United States. One area of ongoing importance to U.S. federal, state, and local policymakers is how to address the critical policy issues accompanying surges in immigration over the U.S. southwest border and the growing number of families and children involved, including the demands placed on public services and options for meeting the needs of these families and their host communities. In particular, the migration of children across the border, whether with their families or unaccompanied, has a considerable impact on K–12 public schools, which are federally required to serve and support these children. Yet sufficient information needed for policymaking is lacking—in particular about ages and geographic locations of the children by state and district, needs for teachers and staff to accommodate the children, and experiences and good practices in schools.

The goal of this report is to understand how states and local communities manage education for undocumented and asylum-seeking children, taking into account various aspects of the children's experiences, from when they cross the border to when they attend schools. It specifically aims to help various stakeholders understand the range of issues related to supporting these children and the schools that educate them. Our research addresses the following questions:

- How many undocumented and asylum-seeking children arrived from FYs 2017 through 2019 in the United States from Mexico and Central America, where are they, and what factors affect how many might arrive over the next several years?
- What are the federal and state policy landscapes for the education of undocumented and asylum-seeking children?
- What approaches are school systems taking for these children's education?
- How can state and local education systems be prepared and supported?

We explore these questions through a rich mix of quantitative and qualitative research: (1) modeling of the numbers and locations of children who have crossed the southwest border from FYs 2017 through 2019 and enrolled in schools, along with implications for new teacher and staff needs; (2) federal and state policy analysis and interviews with officials from federal and state governments and other policy organizations; and (3) interviews and focus groups with administrators and educators supporting undocumented and asylum-seeking children in two case study K–12 school districts. Our intent is for the findings and recommendations stemming from this research to be useful to policymakers and practitioners alike in supporting and educating this population of children in the United States.

In the remainder of this introduction, we provide background to the study by discussing the increase in flows of undocumented and asylum-seeking children over the U.S. southwest border, the reasons for these increased migration flows, and the policy implications of these surges. We then describe our approach and the limitations of the study and provide a road map to the rest of the report.

Migration over the U.S. Southwest Border Is Increasing

There are 50.7 million immigrants in the United States, making the United States home to the largest number of immigrants in the world (International Organization for Migration, 2019). The majority of these immigrants came for work, family, or study reasons and entered with visas through established immigration channels. Estimates of the number of what are often termed by those who monitor these populations as *unauthorized* immigrants in the United States—those who lack official documentation permitting them to live in the United States— range from 10.4 million to 12 million (Baker, 2018; Capps et al., 2020; Passel and Cohn, 2018; Warren, 2021). Roughly half are from Mexico, with about 2 million from Central America and 1.5 million from Asia (Kamarck and Stenglein, 2019b). Of these, most (62 percent) are those who overstayed their visas, while a smaller proportion arrived through crossing the U.S. southwest border (Warren, 2017).

Immigration over the U.S. southwest border has been a source of considerable political controversy in recent years. Discussions of the recent surge have generally focused on three categories of people crossing the border. The first group, called *apprehensions*, consists of individuals who cross the border without valid U.S. immigration or visa documentation and are detained by U.S. Customs and Border Protection (CBP). The second group consists of individuals who arrive at border ports of entry and turn themselves in to CBP to claim asylum; the official term for this group is *inadmissibles*, even though many are admitted to the United States while they wait for their asylum cases to be processed. CBP terms both these first two categories *encounters*. A third group of migrants consists of those who cross the border undetected. This number is difficult to estimate but is probably correlated with the number of apprehensions (Office of Immigration Statistics, 2017). Our discussions include the first two groups, apprehensions and inadmissibles, in some cases focusing on apprehensions because data about inadmissibles are incomplete and do not allow for historical comparisons.

As reflected in Figure 1.1, in FY 2019 the number of apprehensions at the U.S. southwest border reached a 12-year high, at more than 800,000, dropping in FY 2020 because the COVID-19 pandemic. FY 2019's numbers were still only half of those in FY 2000, a peak year with more than 1.6 million apprehensions. That said, FY 2019 saw the largest year-to-year spike in southwest border encounters on record, with the number of apprehensions and inadmissibles totaling more than 977,000 (CBP, 2021).

Furthermore, the profile of arrivals has changed dramatically since 2000. Arrivals once consisted almost exclusively of single adult Mexicans seeking work. In contrast, over 70 percent of arrivals in FY 2019 came from the Central American Northern Triangle countries of Honduras, Guatemala, and El Salvador. Figure 1.1 shows the trends since FY 2000 in the number of individuals apprehended at the southwest border from Mexico (the purple area) versus other countries (the green area); the top of the green area reflects the sum of all apprehensions.

FIGURE 1.1

U.S. Southwest Border Apprehensions of Mexicans and Non-Mexicans, by Fiscal Year

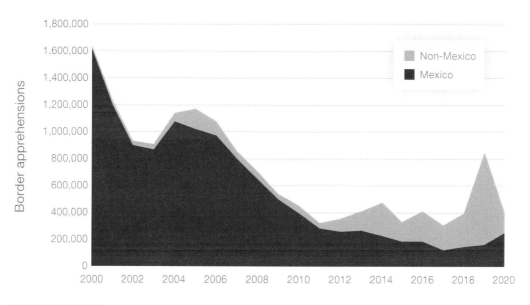

SOURCE: CBP, 2021.

Additionally, a growing number of children have been apprehended at the southwest border, as shown in Figure 1.2. Although most children come as part of family units, there are also significant numbers of unaccompanied children (Gramlich and Noe-Bustamante, 2019; Singer and Kandel, 2019). In FY 2019, more than 473,000 individuals arriving as family units were apprehended, as well as more than 76,000 unaccompanied children ages 17 and younger; another 58,000 unaccompanied children and family units encountered border officials at ports of entry and were deemed inadmissible, which includes those who claimed asylum and entered the United States. The 473,682 people apprehended in family units in FY 2019 represented more than half of all apprehensions in that year, and the number of individuals in this category was more than four times that from the year before—greater than at any point on record. According to CBP data, apprehensions of unaccompanied children also reached their highest level on record in FY 2019, although this group (displayed as the green area in Figure 1.2) was much smaller than the number of people in family units apprehended (the purple area).

At the time of this report, FY 2021 encounters were on target to exceed those of FY 2019, the recent peak, after dropping during FY 2020 due to the pandemic. Figure 1.3 shows monthly CBP southwest border encounters from FY 2018 to FY 2021. There were more than 170,000 encounters in March 2021 alone, in comparison to about 100,000 in March 2019. Unlike in recent previous years, most CBP encounters through April 2021 involved single adults (75 percent), while 16.5 percent involved family units and 8.5 percent involved unaccompanied children (CBP, 2021).

FIGURE 1.2

Southwest Border Apprehensions of Families, Children, and Single Adults, by Fiscal Year

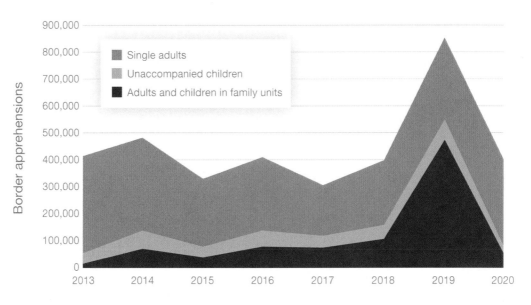

SOURCE: CBP, 2021.

FIGURE 1.3
Southwest Border Encounters by Month

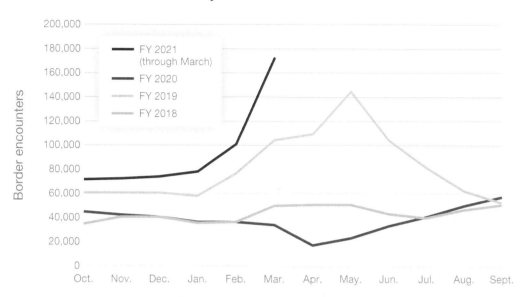

SOURCE: CBP, 2021.

Why Are These Migration Flows of Children Happening?

We now consider what is known about the reasons for the migration of children across the southwest border. There are multiple overlapping factors that contribute to these changing migration patterns, including the larger total numbers of individuals crossing the border and increases in families and children from the Northern Triangle. Many complicated factors within immigrants' home countries serve as push factors, along with pull factors from the United States. There is no scholarly consensus on exact contribution of particular reasons. The factors at play are presented in the following sections.

Violence

In recent years, high levels of violence and intimidation in the Northern Triangle countries (both gang violence and gender based) have contributed to outmigration (Takemoto, 2019). El Salvador, Honduras, and Mexico rank in the top ten countries globally for violent deaths of civilians as a proportion of the population—with fewer deaths proportionately in 2019 than Syria and South Sudan but more than Libya, Yemen, and Iraq, all of which had either ongoing civil wars or high levels of violence from terrorism (Parker, 2020). El Salvador and Honduras have Latin America's highest rates of murders of women and girls (United Nations Economic Commission for Latin America and the Caribbean, undated). Threats of violence, in particular, could be driving families to the border to ensure the safety of all family members.

Poverty and Lack of Economic Opportunity

The Northern Triangle countries rank in the bottom quartile for gross domestic product and have high inequality, with 66 percent of Hondurans and 49 percent of Guatemalans living below the poverty line (Cheatham, 2021; World Bank, undated-a, undated-b). Forty-two percent of people in Mexico are categorized as "multidimensionally poor," according to the World Bank (Inchauste, 2020). Agricultural setbacks have contributed to food insecurity, and, relatedly, the effects of climate change are likely to bring future migration pressures, including lower incomes for workers in the agricultural sector, as global warming and droughts make farming less productive (Lustgarten, 2020). In comparison, many are attracted by plentiful and more-lucrative job opportunities in the United States.

Natural Disasters

In 2020, Hurricanes Eta and Iota devastated regions of Central America that are home to more than 5 million people, spurring migration north to the United States, similar to the effect that Hurricane Mitch had in 1998 (Kitroeff, 2020). United Nations Children's Fund (UNICEF) estimates that, as of January 2021, 4.8 million people, including 1.8 million children, were in need of humanitarian assistance. Thousands of families have lost homes or jobs, leading migrant caravans in some of the worst-hit locations to walk to the United States (UNICEF, 2021).

Poor Governance

Corruption, low tax-collection rates, and lapses in the rule of law in these countries have led to weak economic growth, dependence on remittances, and weak public services. Underfunded state institutions cannot deliver adequate social services to their populations. State institutions also fail to provide adequate government response to frequent natural disasters (Meyer and Taft-Morales, 2019). The increasing flow of migrants and lax rule of law have also increased the supply of people with expertise and experience in human smuggling in support of migration.

Evolving U.S. Policies

Some have attributed surges in the migration of children specifically to incentives provided by U.S. asylum procedures that increasingly benefit minors. For example, there was a surge in child immigrants after the 1997 *Flores* Settlement Agreement, which improved the conditions for minors apprehended at the border (Sussis, 2019). As of 1990, children and some young adults could receive U.S. lawful permanent residence through Special Immigrant Juvenile Status, which applies to minors who are neglected, abused, or abandoned by a parent even if they entered the United States without documentation (Immigration Center for Women and Children, undated). The possibility of a free public school education may incentivize some families to cross the border and ensure that their children receive formal schooling. Yet these policies have been in place for some time. They do not explain the most-recent surges in migration of children in 2019, when the Trump administration specifically focused on policies intended to reduce asylum seeking and benefits for immigrants crossing the border; these included family separations (Gonzalez, 2018) and other policies meant to disincentive border crossings (Amadeo, 2021).

Circumstances Particular to 2021

There is disagreement over the specific causes of the increases in 2021. Reasons have been attributed to pent-up demand for migration after the pandemic, weak economies in Mexico and Central America because of the pandemic, poor recovery efforts after Hurricanes Eta and Iota, perceptions by migrants of more open-migration policies in general from the Biden administration, the Biden administration's decision to admit unaccompanied children, and typical seasonal patterns that show increased migration during the winter months when desert-crossing conditions are less treacherous (Chiacu, 2021; Gramlich, 2021; Wong, De Roche, and Venzor, 2021). The COVID-19 pandemic has worsened the economies of Central America and Mexico, while the recovering U.S. economy provides attraction.

What Are the Policy Implications of Large Surges in Immigrant Children?

Drawing on U.S. Census Bureau data through 2018, the Migration Policy Institute estimated that U.S. schools were serving 737,000 undocumented children (ages 3 through 17), representing previous migration waves and every country of origin (Migration Policy Institute, undated). These estimates include both people who crossed the U.S. southwest border without documentation and people who overstayed their visas. However, this does not include recent years and does not focus exclusively on those who have crossed the border either undocumented or seeking asylum.

Regardless of why surges in the migration of children are happening, they have considerable implications for both the children who are arriving in the United States and those who are called on to support them. U.S. public schools are federally required to educate all children regardless of immigration status and cannot require students or parents to disclose or document their immigration status (*Plyler v. Doe*, 1982). Recent education policies have also required states to adopt English-language proficiency policies aligned with academic standards so that all children have access to those rigorous standards (Lee, 2018). Schools may need to address multiple challenges, as many undocumented and asylum-seeking children are English-language learners (ELLs), might have missed several years of school or are academically behind, are often placed into new families as sponsors, are in impoverished households, or have symptoms of psychological distress and trauma (Camarota, Griffith, and Zeigler, 2017; Cardoza, 2019; McDonnell and Hill, 1993; Pivovarova and Powers, 2019). We will explore these issues later in this report.

A Note on Terminology

A challenge we encountered is the lack of an accurate and neutral term for the population of children considered in this study. Therefore, we decided on the long phrase *undocumented and asylum-seeking children* for our general use in this report. In some specific cases, we also use other terms. We use the term *unauthorized* when referring to some data, as that is how those particular data sources are labeled, as well as some discussion of laws that use that term. In discussions of the case studies in our two school districts, we also use the terms *newcomer* and *English-language learner* (ELL). Below are considerations that went into this use of terminology.

First, there is no single term for this population of children because it includes several groups who have crossed the border and whom we are putting together in this context: those who applied for asylum, those who received asylum, those who were apprehended at the border, and those who crossed the border undetected.

Second, available legal definitions either are not specific to the population we are studying or have negative connotations that might not be appropriate for referring to children. Definitions in the Immigration and Naturalization Act to describe foreign-born populations residing in the United States include the following (Pub. L. 82-414, 1952):

- An **immigrant** is a foreign national lawfully admitted to the United States for permanent residence.
- A **refugee** or **asylee** is an individual fleeing their country because of persecution, or a "well-founded" fear of persecution, on account of race, religion, nationality, membership in a particular social group, or political opinion.
- An **unauthorized alien** (a foreign national who resides unlawfully in the United States and who entered the United States "without inspection" (i.e., illegally) or "with inspection" (i.e., lawfully) but violated the terms of admission.

Although some of the children discussed in this report include *unauthorized aliens* according to the U.S. legal definitions, the term *unauthorized alien* to refer to children has negative connotations and is not necessarily accurate in the context of education, as federal law provides authorization for all children in the United States, regardless of immigration status, to receive public schooling (Kwan, 2021).

Third, although there are other terms available, none of them fit our purposes exactly. Many demographic studies use the term *unauthorized immigrant* (e.g., Hoefer, Rytina, and Baker, 2012; Passel and Cohn, 2011), but the term *undocumented* is often used in academic literature related to education and health (Enriquez, 2011; Gonzales, Suárez-Orozco, and Dedios-Sanguineti, 2013; Marshall et al., 2005). *Undocumented* is also a term widely used in the media for those who have crossed the border undetected, but it does not include those who are in asylum processing who are also included in our study. The Biden administration announced a preferred term of *undocumented noncitizens* (Rose, 2021). The United Nations uses the term *undocumented, nondocumented,* or *irregular* to refer to people "who do not fulfil the requirements established by the country of destination to enter, stay or exercise an economic activity" (United Nations High Commissioner for Refugees, 2018). The European Union often refers to people similarly entering those countries as *irregular migrants.*

Fourth, school leaders and state officials interviewed for this study often used the terms *newcomers* or *English language learners.* However, these terms also include others who are not part of our study. The term *newcomer* also includes students new to the United States with immigration visas. ELLs can include the population of our study and citizens or immigrants with visas who are ELLs and have similar needs. Some types of federal funding are also provided for ELLs who are included in our population of study.

Study Approach

This study used the following approaches.

We modeled the population of undocumented and asylum-seeking children in the United States. We estimated the size of this population, its distribution across the country, the portion of this population of children who are enrolled in school systems, and implications for teacher and staffing needs. We bounded our analysis by focusing on arrivals to the border over the FYs 2017–2019 period from Mexico and the Northern Triangle countries of El Salvador, Guatemala, and Honduras, which accounted for more than 90 percent of child migrants in these years (a larger share than of the adult migrant population). Our starting point for this analysis was the U.S. Department of Homeland Security (DHS) Enforcement Lifecycle data as of March 2020 on the status of individuals encountered at the southwest border over these three years, by nationality and family status. We drew directly on DHS data on unaccompanied children and estimated the share of individuals encountered in family units who were children, with data made available by the Transactional Records Access Clearinghouse. Three measures contributed to our modeling of where children are living: Migration Policy Institute estimates of where undocumented immigrants from Mexico and Central America live, U.S. Department of Health and Human Services (HHS) Office of Refugee Resettlement (ORR) records of where unaccompanied children are placed with sponsors, and immigration court data on where child cases are located. We generated counts of children enrolled in school by estimating the age distribution of the migrant children and the share by age of those who enroll in school. Last, we drew on data from the National Center for Education Statistics (NCES) on the demographic characteristics of schools, as well as student-teacher ratios, to estimate impacts on state and county school systems and implications for staffing. For details of our modeling approach, see the appendix.

We examined the federal and state policy contexts. We relied on two data collection and analysis strategies to understand the policy context. We engaged in more comprehensive inquiry regarding federal policy, taking a temporally open-ended approach. We did a more limited examination of the state policy context, focusing on the most recent five years (2016 to 2021) to build understanding and explore the implications of federalism for this population. First, we reviewed available legislation and academic and grey literature about federal and state policies, impacts of various policy tools, and federal and state considerations for educating this population. Our review involved compiling potentially relevant federal policies using resources on federal and state agency websites, resources from the National Conference of State Legislatures, and research literature regarding the history and effects of federal policy on the education of this population. Second, we conducted interviews (both in-person and virtually) with 12 federal, state, and academic stakeholders, including the U.S. Department of Education, Democratic and Republican House of Representatives and Senate staff working on these issues, state education agency (SEA) officials, education-oriented nonprofit organizations, and academics. Our interviews and subsequent analysis provided key-informant perspectives on the implications of these policies for the population and pointed us toward additional policies and guidance, which we synthesized for this report.

We conducted case studies of two school systems' policies and practices for incorporating and accommodating undocumented and asylum-seeking children from Central America and Mexico. The two case studies focused on students' educational experiences in two very different contexts: Jefferson Parish Schools in Louisiana and Oakland Unified School District in California. We selected these case studies to include one district that experienced large, recent increases in the population of children in this study (Jefferson Parish) and include a second district that has been serving large numbers of these children for many years (Oakland Unified). Both are in the top ten states and top 40 districts nationally in terms of numbers of newly arriving students. One is in a sanctuary state; California's 2017 "sanctuary law" prevents local law enforcement from assisting federal immigration enforcement agencies in detaining and transferring undocumented immigrants (Bojórquez, 2020). One is not (Louisiana). We conducted interviews or focus groups with nearly 40 staff across these two case study districts, including district and school leaders, district administrative staff with responsibilities related to this population, teachers in newcomer programs, English as a second language (ESL) teachers, coaches of teachers with newcomer students, and counselors in three schools within each district (one elementary school, one middle school, and one high school). Individuals were chosen for the interviews as follows: Our team requested to talk to teachers and staff working with this population in one elementary, one middle, and one high school to district leadership, which selected schools and delegated choice of interviewees to the principals.

To analyze our interview data, we developed an initial coding scheme based on emergent themes gleaned from the interviews, and then revised this scheme over the course of the coding process. We coded the interviews from each case study district separately, on the basis of our initial coding scheme, and developed additional codes for emergent themes throughout the coding process. We then reviewed the coding to develop cross-case themes.

Limitations

This study has several limitations.

First, the study started prior to the COVID-19 pandemic and was completed during the pandemic. This meant that the data about arrivals on the southwest border in 2019, 2020, and 2021 are not following established patterns; circumstances may further change significantly in coming years in unanticipated ways. Some interviews were conducted prior to the pandemic, and some were conducted during the pandemic, which might have led to differing perspectives on the relative importance of various issues discussed in the report. Our case studies with the districts in California and Louisiana had initially been planned as in-person visits; due to the pandemic, they were conducted online as interviews and focus groups.

Second, several assumptions and limitations of our modeling approach merit mention. Our estimates counted only children who we could observe in the data. As a result, children crossing the border without encountering a CBP official (e.g., undetected entrants) were excluded. In tandem with our focus on Mexico and the Northern Triangle countries, from which most but not all children crossing the border in recent years have come, our models may underestimate the numbers of children in some cases. On the other hand, the DHS data we drew on to estimate children remaining in undocumented status in the United States might not capture those who leave the United States undetected, and, additionally, Enforcement Lifecycle data are event based rather than individual based and may result in some children being counted more than once. Furthermore, the data contributing to our estimates of the distribution of children across the country do not include information on many counties because of small sample sizes, resulting in our being unable to distribute some share of arrivals across those counties. These and other assumptions and limitations of our modeling approach are described in the appendix.

Third, the qualitative trends we identified through our case study investigation were necessarily limited by the numbers and range of interviewees with whom we were able to speak, as well as the limitations of focusing only on two school districts among the more than 13,000 school districts across the United States. In particular, interviews did not include teachers of mainstream classes with newcomer students in them, parents of newcomers' teachers, or newcomer students themselves, and our analysis is therefore missing these perspectives. We include better understanding these perspectives in our recommendations at the end of this report.

A Road Map of This Report

The remainder of this report is organized as follows:

- Chapter Two provides an analysis of how many undocumented and asylum-seeking children there are and in which states and counties they reside.
- Chapter Three provides an overview of the federal and state policy landscapes for the education of undocumented and asylum-seeking children.
- Chapter Four presents our findings from case studies of a school district in California and a school district in Louisiana.
- Chapter Five concludes with policy implications and recommendations.
- The appendix provides details of our modeling approach for estimating the number and geographic location of the children, as well as detailed data tables.

CHAPTER TWO

The Number and Locations of the Undocumented and Asylum-Seeking Children

Although the recent surge from undocumented and asylum-seeking children arriving to the southwest border is well established, data that track these children from the border to local communities and ultimately K–12 public schools are not available to the extent needed to support policymaking. In particular, data on whether unaccompanied children and children in family units encountered at the border remain in the country in unresolved status do not include the locations or ages of these recent arrivals. Meanwhile, estimates of the size of the undocumented population overall that draw on data from the U.S. Census Bureau and other sources are not timely enough to account to meet the needs of policymakers.

In this chapter, we discuss the results of our modeling regarding the number; age distribution; location of undocumented and asylum-seeking children entering the United States from FYs 2017 through 2019 via the southwest border from Mexico and the Northern Triangle countries of El Salvador, Guatemala, and Honduras; and implications for teacher and staffing needs. We call this population of undocumented and asylum-seeking children who arrived from FYs 2017 through 2019 *recent arrivals*. First, we present our overall national findings for arrivals from this period. Next, we discuss where these children are located to understand where impacts on state and county school systems are most likely concentrated and what the approximate magnitude of those impacts is both in numerical terms and as a share of the baseline population. We conclude by discussing how variation in both the flow of migrant children to the border and policy factors can affect the number of future arrivals that can be expected in schools, as well as how local education policymakers could look to real-time measures of border encounters as a leading indicator of what to expect in their communities in the near to medium term.

We note that we do not provide estimates for arrivals during FY 2020. This is because of the data sources we drew on for our estimates, in particular a DHS report for which FY 2019 was the last complete year of data, and the unique circumstances of the COVID-19 pandemic. See the appendix for additional details on our data sources and methods.

National Estimates of Recent Arrivals

We estimate that nearly 575,000 children (half a million children from the Northern Triangle and 75,000 children from Mexico) encountered CBP officials at the southwest border over the FYs 2017–2019 period. These four countries accounted for 93 percent of all CBP encounters with children from any country over that period. Of these children, we estimate that roughly 491,000 (or 86 percent of arrivals from these countries) remained in the United States in unresolved status as of March 2020. These totals include both unaccompanied children and children in family units.[1] Here, we describe step by step how we developed these estimates.

Table 2.1 displays encounters with children by year, country of origin, and category of child (i.e., unaccompanied or in family units). Overall, children in family units outnumbered unaccompanied children roughly two to one. There was a surge of encounters with children in FY 2019, similar to overall trends at the border, shown in Chapter One. In particular, children in family units from the Northern Triangle arriving in FY 2019 accounted for more than 40 percent of the three-year total of arriving children.

Table 2.2 presents our estimates of how many of these children remained in the United States in unresolved status as of March 2020. We derive these estimates from data published by the DHS Office of Immigration Statistics in its *Fiscal Year 2020 Enforcement Lifecycle Report*, which links administrative records across previously siloed DHS and U.S. Department of Justice (DOJ) data (Rosenblum and Zhang, 2020). The share of children remaining in the United States in unresolved status is larger for more-recent years of arrival, as recent arrivals have had less time to be processed through the system. Yet even for FY 2017, more than half of unaccompanied children and nearly 90 percent of children in family units encountered are estimated to remain in the country in unresolved status as of March 2020. Children from the Northern Triangle not only account for the vast majority of encounters over the FYs 2017–2019 period but also are much more likely than children from Mexico to have remained in the United States in unresolved status. This owes in part to differences in how children are processed at the border: Unaccompanied children from Mexico, for example, often voluntarily return to Mexico, an option used only for unaccompanied children from contiguous countries (Smith, 2019, p. 25).

Figure 2.1 shows our estimates of the status of children encountered at the southwest border over the FYs 2017–2019 period, using data in the DHS report (Rosenblum and Zhang, 2020), with the vast majority (86 percent) remaining in the United States in unresolved status. Encounters that are *unresolved* and where there is *no confirmed departure* form the basis of

---

[1] We assume that 54 percent of individuals in family units from the Northern Triangle countries and 56 percent from Mexico are children, shares we estimated using CBP data made available by the Transactional Records Access Clearinghouse (TRAC). The data include the countries of origin and ages of those apprehended and separately identify children and adults in family units. The TRAC data also include FY 2017 apprehensions data through July 2017 and FY 2018 data through April 2018. For simplicity, we apply these shares to all encounters (i.e., both apprehensions and inadmissibles) for FYs 2017–2019 (TRAC Reports, undated-a).

TABLE 2.1

Southwest Border Encounters, by Country of Origin and Family Status, FYs 2017–2019

Country of Origin	FY 2017		FY 2018		FY 2019		Total, FYs 2017–2019		
	Children in Family Units	Unaccompanied Children	Children in Family Units	Unaccompanied Children	Children in Family Units	Unaccompanied Children	Children in Family Units	Unaccompanied Children	Total Children
El Salvador	15,291	10,852	9,400	5,782	31,513	12,161	56,204	28,795	85,000
Guatemala	16,586	17,623	33,796	26,018	102,430	30,996	152,812	74,637	227,400
Honduras	14,139	8,936	25,794	12,568	104,343	20,929	144,276	42,433	186,700
Total, Northern Triangle	45,980	37,346	68,942	44,336	237,933	64,065	352,855	145,747	498,600
Mexico	5,776	10,206	12,797	12,346	19,666	13,445	39,655	35,997	75,700
Total, Northern Triangle and Mexico	51,756	47,552	81,739	56,682	257,598	77,510	392,510	181,744	574,300
All countries, southwest border	56,705	48,626	87,098	58,668	284,590	80,636	428,393	187,930	616,300
% Northern Triangle	81%	77%	79%	76%	84%	79%	82%	78%	81%
% Mexico	10%	21%	15%	21%	7%	17%	9%	19%	12%
% Northern Triangle and Mexico	91%	98%	94%	97%	91%	96%	92%	97%	93%

SOURCES: Rosenblum and Zhang, 2020; CBP, 2021; TRAC Reports, undated-a.

NOTES: El Salvador, Guatemala, and Honduras data are taken from DHS data sources other than the *Fiscal Year 2020 Enforcement Lifecycle Report*, and the individual country-level data do not sum to the total for the Northern Triangle countries in that report; children in family units are estimated to be 54 percent of family units overall and for family units from Northern Triangle countries, and 56 percent of family units from Mexico, according to our analysis of TRAC data. Estimates of total children are rounded to the nearest hundred.

TABLE 2.2

Estimated Number of Recently Arrived Children in the United States in Unresolved Status in March 2020, Mexico and Northern Triangle Countries, by Family Status, FYs 2017–2019

Nationality	FY 2017		FY 2018		FY 2019		Total, FYs 2017–2019		
	Children in Family Units	Unaccompanied Children	Children in Family Units	Unaccompanied Children	Children in Family Units	Unaccompanied Children	Children in Family Units	Unaccompanied Children	Total Children
Number of children									
Northern Triangle	42,600	26,300	65,600	37,700	227,100	61,200	335,200	125,200	460,400
Mexico	2,900	700	9,000	1,200	15,600	1,400	27,500	3,300	30,800
Northern Triangle and Mexico	45,500	27,000	74,600	39,000	242,700	62,600	362,700	128,500	491,200
Share of encounters									
Northern Triangle	93%	70%	95%	85%	95%	96%	95%	86%	92%
Mexico	48%	7%	68%	10%	76%	11%	69%	9%	41%
Northern Triangle and Mexico	87%	57%	91%	69%	94%	81%	92%	71%	86%

SOURCES: Rosenblum and Zhang, 2020; TRAC Reports, undated-a.

NOTES: Estimates of children remaining in the country in unresolved status include children with no confirmed departure according to the DHS *Enforcement Lifecycle Report* (Rosenblum and Zhang, 2020), with the exception of children who have been granted relief. We apply the same assumptions as in Table 2.1 to estimate the share of individuals in family units who are children and make a further assumption that the March 2020 status of individuals in family units does not vary for adults versus children. All numbers and totals are rounded to the nearest hundred.

FIGURE 2.1

Recently Arrived Undocumented and Asylum-Seeking Children, Mexico and Northern Triangle, by Fiscal Year of Arrival, Category of Child, and Status as of March 2020, FYs 2017–2019

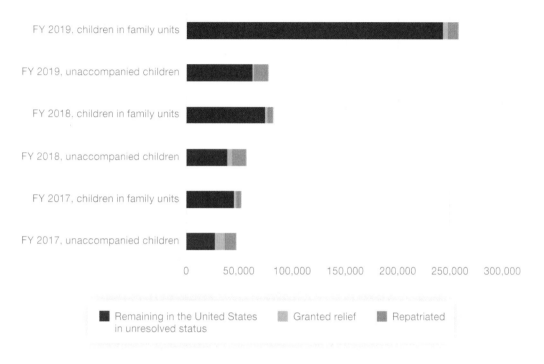

SOURCES: Authors' calculations based on data from Rosenblum and Zhang, 2020, and TRAC Reports, undated-a.
NOTES: Arrivals reflect all CBP encounters at the southwest border, including apprehensions and inadmissibility determinations and including an adjustment based on TRAC data to estimate the share of family units who are children. We assume that the distribution of status as of March 2020 is the same for children in family units as for all individuals arriving as part of family units. Data are event based, so children encountered on multiple occasions are counted each time.

these estimates. Our estimates do not include encounters that are *resolved* with a migrant *repatriated*, nor do they include encounters that are *resolved* with *no confirmed departure*, as these encounters resulted in a *grant of relief* (e.g., asylum) that conveys legal status to remain in the United States. The DHS report (and Figure 2.1) does not assign encounters to the category of *unresolved* and *repatriated*.[2]

---

[2] We note that some portion of children in family units with unresolved statuses might have been outside the country as of March 2020 if they were processed through the Migrant Protection Protocols (MPP), or "Remain in Mexico," which was implemented midway through FY 2019. According to the U.S. Government Accountability Office (2020), by the end of FY 2019, 30,100 family unit members were processed through MPP. This suggests that approximately 16,000 to 17,000 children that we include in our "in-country, undocumented" group might have been outside the country in March 2020. Beginning February 2021, individuals who had been processed through MPP and with pending immigration proceedings before the Executive Office of Immigration Review (EOIR) have been processed into the United States.

In estimating the number of children remaining in the country in unresolved status, we made several simplifying assumptions.[3] These assumptions could mean that our estimates either overcount or undercount the actual number.

Assumptions that might lead to an *overcount* are as follows. DHS notes in its report that *no confirmed departure* should be interpreted as "likely remains in the United States," which we have done here (Rosenblum and Zhang, 2020). However, some of those with *no confirmed departure* might not remain in the United States, as "an unknown share" of individuals with this status "may have departed the United States without notifying DHS." For example, if everyone who received a final removal order or agreed to depart voluntarily did indeed depart, our estimate of the number of recently arrived children remaining in the country would be about 20 percent lower. Moreover, DHS data reflect "event cycles" or the number of encounters, not the numbers of individual children. That means that children who have come in and out of the United States could be encountered multiple times at the border, so they could be counted multiple times in the data.[4]

Conversely, our estimates may be an *undercount* because we do not include children who entered the country illegally *without encountering CBP agents*. DHS sources suggest that the magnitude of this undercount is not large. For example, the DHS *Border Security Metrics Report* assumes that children and family units make no effort to evade detection (preferring to turn themselves in to claim asylum) and have an apprehension rate of 100 percent (i.e., they are all included in apprehensions counts and none enter undetected) (DHS, 2019b).[5] However, it seems unlikely that CBP apprehends all the children who cross the border and therefore likely that we are missing some portion of these children. Additionally, we considered children only from Mexico and the Northern Triangle countries and not other countries.[6]

We note that the methods we used to derive our estimates of the number of undocumented and asylum-seeking children in the United States differ from those used by other researchers because of the very specific population we are estimating—recent arrivals crossing the southwest border and remaining in the United States as of early 2020. We do not

---

[3] In addition to the assumptions described in these paragraphs, we assume that the distribution of statuses as of March 2020 is the same for children in family units as for all individuals arriving as part of family units. The DHS report does not provide separate data for children and adults in family units (Rosenblum and Zhang, 2020).

[4] In the DHS *Enforcement Lifecycle Report*, a *reencounter* of the same child at the border results in the initial encounter being designated as *resolved* with the migrant *repatriated* (and hence removed from our estimates of children remaining in the country) (Rosenblum and Zhang, 2020). This factor mitigates the degree to which this factor leads to an overcount.

[5] Specifically, children and family units are considered "non-impactable" by "traditional enforcement policies" because "even if they are apprehended they are typically unlikely to be immediately removed or returned" (DHS, 2019b, pp. 7–8; Office of Immigration Statistics, 2017, pp. 17–18).

[6] Because the data sources we drew on to estimate the distribution of children across states and counties frequently relied on data at the country-of-origin level, we focused on Mexico and Northern Triangle countries and did not replicate the calculations for countries of origin that collectively accounted for less than 10 percent of children encountered at the border.

consider visa overstayers, nor do we account for reverse flows of earlier arrivals who might have exited the country over the FYs 2017–2019 period. Other researchers who estimate the undocumented population often use what are known as *residual-based* methods that combine data from the U.S. Census Bureau and other sources to estimate the undocumented (or unauthorized) population as the difference between the total immigrant population and the legal immigrant population. As discussed in Chapter One, estimates of the total number of these immigrants—including children and adults from all countries and both border crossers and visa overstayers—range from about 10.4 million to about 12.0 million and reflect the number in the country as of 2015 to mid-2019 (Baker, 2018; Capps et al., 2020; Passel and Cohn, 2018; Warren, 2021).

Estimated Age Distribution and Share Enrolled in School

Of the total of 491,200 children arriving over the FYs 2017–2019 period and remaining in the United States, we estimate that about 321,000 attended K–12 schools during the 2019–2020 school year. This takes into consideration their age distribution upon arrival (as shown in Figure 2.2), "ages forward" the children by one to three years depending on their year of arrival, and applies assumptions about the share of children in each age group in schools.[7] Totals are shown in Table 2.3. This represents a little under two-thirds (65 percent) of the number of the child arrivals we estimate to be in the country and about 56 percent of the roughly 574,000 CBP encounters of children from these countries over the years of interest.

We also point out the marked difference in the age distribution between unaccompanied children and children who arrive with a parent or guardian. As shown in Figure 2.2, most children arriving in family units (77 percent) were younger (age 12 or younger), while most unaccompanied children (74 percent) were teenagers ages 15 to 17.[8] These differences affect how many we expect to be in K–12 schools. Some children arriving with their families are not yet of elementary-school age, while many unaccompanied children arrived as teenagers, are now age 18 or older, and may be more likely to be in the workforce or possibly postsecondary schools than in the K–12 system.

---

[7] Our assumptions regarding the share of children in schools by age group are derived from aggregate data on the share of "unauthorized" children in school published by the Migration Policy Institute (undated). The Migration Policy Institute data suggest that most K–12 school-age undocumented and asylum-seeking children do attend school, albeit at a somewhat lower rate than NCES data show for the overall population of children. Note that the Migration Policy Institute refers to this population as "unauthorized."

[8] The estimated age shares reflect averages over FY 2015 to FY 2018 for children from Mexico and the Northern Triangle countries. The TRAC data tool we used to make the estimates allowed for parsing by country of origin, category of child (unaccompanied or children in family units), and age; parsing by fiscal year of arrival in addition to these factors was impractical, nor do we believe it would have led to meaningful differences (TRAC Reports undated-a). For example, data from the ORR show that there has been little variation over time in the age distribution of unaccompanied children (ORR, 2021).

FIGURE 2.2

Share of Undocumented and Asylum-Seeking Children, by Age Group, Mexico and Northern Triangle, FYs 2015–2018

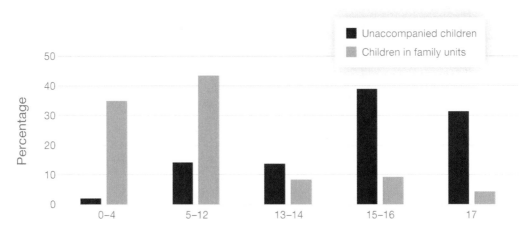

SOURCE: Authors' calculations based on data from TRAC Reports, undated-a.

NOTES: Age shares are calculated by summing the number of children from each of the three Northern Triangle countries in each age group and category of child (i.e., unaccompanied and children in family units) identified in the TRAC apprehensions data over the FYs 2015–2018 period. We assume that the shares for inadmissibles (and therefore for all border encounters) are identical.

TABLE 2.3

Estimated Number of Recently Arrived Undocumented and Asylum-Seeking Children in the United States and in K–12 Education Systems, as of March 2020, Mexico and Northern Triangle, by Age Group

	Ages 1–4	Ages 5–12	Ages 13–17	Age 18	Ages 19–20	Total
Mexico	6,300	14,300	6,500	2,100	1,500	30,800
Northern Triangle	76,800	177,900	125,900	46,800	33,000	460,400
Total	83,100	192,200	132,400	48,900	34,500	491,200
Assumed share in school	0%	90%	90%	50%	13%	N/A
Total, in school	0	173,000	119,200	24,500	4,300	321,000

SOURCE: Authors' estimates; see the appendix for details on methods and assumptions.

NOTES: Numbers are derived by multiplying the estimated share of child migrants in each age group—estimated separately for Mexico and the Northern Triangle and by category of child (i.e., unaccompanied children and children in family units)—by the estimated number of recently arrived migrant children in that same location-of-origin category of child group. Next, we sum within age groups across Mexico and the Northern Triangle and multiply by the assumed share of children in that age group in school. All numbers are rounded to the nearest hundred. N/A = not applicable.

Estimated Geographic Distribution and Impacts on State and County School Systems

Some states and localities are experiencing larger volumes of recently arrived undocumented and asylum-seeking children (newcomers) than other places. The map in Figure 2.3 shows that each of the three large border states—California, Florida, and Texas—as well as New York—is home to more than 20,000 of these children. More than 10,000 live in each of five East Coast states—Georgia, Maryland, New Jersey, North Carolina, and Virginia. These nine states plus Louisiana (which has 9,200) account for about 75 percent of recent arrivals, according to our estimates.

Relative to the baseline number of Hispanic students, the largest share of recently arrived undocumented and asylum-seeking children are in Louisiana and Maryland, where these children represent more than 10 percent of the baseline Hispanic student population, as shown in Figure 2.4. In Virginia and Georgia, recently arrived undocumented and asylum-seeking children represent both a high absolute number of students (more than 10,000 in each state) and a high share of the baseline Hispanic student population (more than 5 percent). Other locations where recently arrived undocumented and asylum-seeking children account for more than 5 percent of the baseline Hispanic student population—Tennessee, Kentucky,

FIGURE 2.3

Estimated Distribution Across States of Recently Arrived Undocumented and Asylum-Seeking Children from Mexico and the Northern Triangle in Primary- and Secondary-School Systems, as of March 2020

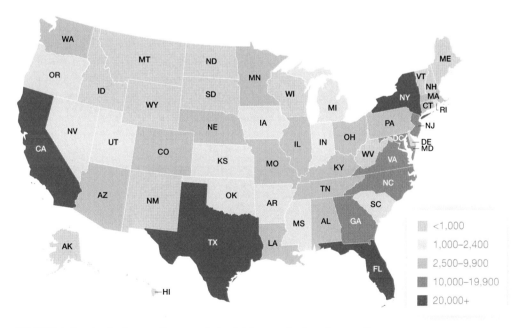

SOURCE: Authors' estimates; see the appendix for details on methods and assumptions.

FIGURE 2.4

Estimated Distribution Across States of Recently Arrived Undocumented and Asylum-Seeking Children from Mexico and the Northern Triangle as a Share of the Baseline Hispanic Population in Primary- and Secondary-School Systems, as of March 2020

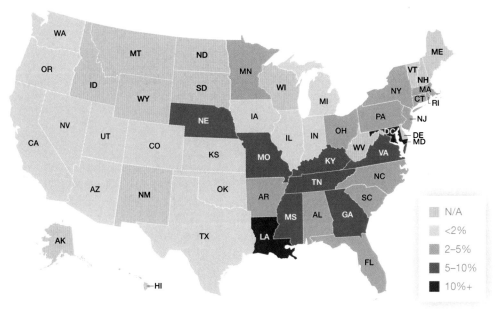

SOURCE: Authors' estimates; see the appendix for details on methods and assumptions.
NOTE: *N/A* (not available) indicates the inability to reliably estimate a percentage because there are fewer than 1,000 children.

Missouri, Mississippi, Nebraska, and the District of Columbia—are not among the top ten by total number due to their smaller by comparison baseline Hispanic student populations. Meanwhile, the four states with the largest numbers of recently arrived undocumented and asylum-seeking children—California, Texas, Florida, and New York—do not crack the top ten in terms of relative share because of their large baseline populations of Hispanic students.

Our estimates of the distribution of children across the states draw on three data sources:

- Migration Policy Institute–provided data on the distribution of the unauthorized (i.e., undocumented) population from Mexico and Central America derived from 2012–2016 U.S. Census Bureau American Community Survey data (see the appendix for more details)
- data from the HHS ORR on where unaccompanied children have been placed with sponsors (Administration for Children and Families, 2021a, 2021b)
- DOJ EOIR immigration court data from TRAC on the location of juvenile cases (TRAC Reports, undated-b).

We weight these three data sources equally to derive our estimates of the state-level distribution of these children, estimating separate distributions where feasible for children from the Northern Triangle versus from Mexico. To estimate the county-level distribution, we rely on the first two sources only. See the appendix for additional details on the data sources, assumptions, and limitations of our modeling approach.

Tables 2.4 and 2.5 provide additional details on the distribution of recently arrived undocumented and asylum-seeking children across states and counties. Specifically, they present information on this group *as a percentage* of enrolled children at baseline (i.e., prior to their arrival)—overall and for several groups into which the recent arrivals likely fit: Hispanic students, limited English proficiency (LEP) or ELL students, and students receiving free or reduced-price lunches (FRL). The data on relative impacts complement the information provided on raw counts of students and shed light on where impacts on school systems may be large in proportional terms. We also estimate the number of additional teachers and other school staff needed to accommodate the recent arrivals while holding student-teacher and student-staff ratios constant, assuming for illustrative purposes that the student population would have held steady in the absence of the recent arrivals. Tables 2.4 and 2.5 display the top ten states and counties by number of children; in the appendix, we present the same data for all states and counties that are home to at least 1,000 recently arrived children and discuss the trade-offs for planners of focusing on raw counts versus relative shares.

New undocumented and asylum-seeking arrivals as a share of baseline student enrollment reach 1 percent in half of the top ten states by number of recent arrivals: Maryland (1.9 percent), Virginia (1.4 percent), Louisiana (1.3 percent), Florida (1.1 percent), and New Jersey (1.0 percent). The shares are larger relative to baseline levels of Hispanic, LEP or ELL, and FRL students. Newly arrived undocumented and asylum-seeking children represent more than 5 percent of the baseline Hispanic student population in four states in the top ten by number of arrivals—Georgia, Louisiana, Maryland, and Virginia. We note that they represent more than 20 percent of the baseline Hispanic student population in Louisiana and more than 10 percent in Maryland. The recent arrivals are more than 5 percent of the baseline LEP or ELL population in all states in the top ten for which data are available, except California. The shares are typically lower relative to FRL students but are at least 2 percent in four states (Louisiana, Maryland, New Jersey, and Virginia) and at least 1 percent in all ten.

We estimate that seven states would each have needed to hire at least 1,000 additional teachers and at least 1,000 additional other staff to support newly arrived undocumented and asylum-seeking children without increasing student-teacher or student-staff ratios. This assumes that the student population in these states otherwise would have remained constant and also that the states do not absorb the new students by allowing student-teacher and student-staff ratios to rise rather than by adding teachers and staff to hold the ratios constant. We expect that the more concentrated the impacts within states, the more likely affected school systems would be to hire additional personnel to meet the increased demand for services. In addition to demands on teachers and staff, school systems in areas with large

TABLE 2.4

Estimated State-Level Impacts of Recently Arrived Undocumented and Asylum-Seeking Children from Mexico and the Northern Triangle on Primary and Secondary School Systems, as of March 2020—States with 1,000 or More Recent Arrivals

State	Number of Children in School	Share of Recent Arrivals	Share of Baseline Students, Overall	Share of Baseline Students, Hispanic	Share of Baseline Students, LEP or ELL	Share of Baseline Students, FRL	Additional Teachers Needed	Additional Other Staff Needed
California	51,600	16.1%	0.8%	1.5%	4.1%	1.4%	2,250	2,720
Texas	48,200	15.0%	0.9%	1.7%	5.2%	1.5%	3,170	3,180
Florida	29,900	9.3%	1.1%	3.3%	10.4%	1.8%	1,980	1,760
New York	23,800	7.4%	0.9%	3.3%	—	1.7%	1,820	1,550
Virginia	18,500	5.8%	1.4%	9.5%	18.3%	3.5%	1,310	1,270
Maryland	16,900	5.3%	1.9%	11.6%	24.5%	4.1%	1,140	1,110
New Jersey	14,700	4.6%	1.0%	3.8%	—	2.8%	1,210	1,270
Georgia	13,600	4.2%	0.8%	5.1%	11.9%	1.2%	880	880
North Carolina	12,900	4.0%	0.8%	4.9%	13.9%	1.4%	830	770
Louisiana	9,200	2.9%	1.3%	20.2%	—	2.0%	620	630

SOURCE: Authors' estimates; see the appendix for details on methods and assumptions.

NOTES: – = missing in underlying data source. "Number of Children in School" is the estimated number of recently arrived undocumented and asylum-seeking children in schools (rounded to the nearest hundred). "Share of Recent Arrivals" is the share of the total estimate of 321,000 arrivals nationwide in the state (derived from unrounded numbers). "Share of Baseline Students" columns indicate these arrivals as a share of baseline public school enrollment in the state, specifically of overall enrollment, Hispanic enrollment, LEP or ELL enrollment, and FRL enrollment. The estimated number of additional teachers and additional other staff needed to accommodate these arrivals (rounded to the nearest ten) reflects the numbers of these personnel needed to maintain baseline student-teacher and student-overall staff ratios, assuming that the enrolled population otherwise would have held steady.

TABLE 2.5

Estimated County-Level Impacts of Recently Arrived Undocumented and Asylum-Seeking Children from Mexico and the Northern Triangle on Primary and Secondary School Systems, as of December 2019—Top 25 Counties by Estimated Number of Children

County	State	Number of Children in School	Share of Recent Arrivals	Share of Baseline Students, Overall	Share of Baseline Students, Hispanic	Share of Baseline Students, FRL	Additional Teachers Needed
Los Angeles County	California	30,400	9.5%	2.0%	3.1%	3.0%	1,300
Harris County	Texas	19,900	6.2%	2.2%	3.9%	3.4%	1,220
Miami-Dade County	Florida	9,300	2.9%	2.6%	3.7%	3.7%	530
Prince George's County	Maryland	7,600	2.4%	5.8%	18.6%	8.6%	520
Dallas County	Texas	6,600	2.1%	1.3%	2.4%	1.8%	420
Suffolk County	New York	6,200	1.9%	2.6%	8.9%	6.9%	440
Montgomery County	Maryland	6,100	1.9%	3.8%	12.8%	11.0%	400
Fairfax County	Virginia	6,100	1.9%	3.4%	13.3%	12.5%	410
Palm Beach County	Florida	5,900	1.8%	3.0%	9.1%	5.2%	400
Nassau County	New York	5,000	1.5%	2.4%	9.9%	8.6%	380

SOURCE: Authors' estimates; see the appendix for details on methods and assumptions.

NOTES: "Number of Children in School" is the estimated number of recently arrived undocumented and asylum-seeking children in schools (rounded to the nearest hundred). "Share of Recent Arrivals" is the share of the total estimate of 321,000 arrivals nationwide in the county (derived from unrounded numbers). "Share of Baseline Students" columns indicate these arrivals as a share of baseline public school enrollment in the state, specifically of overall enrollment, Hispanic enrollment, and FRL enrollment. The estimated number of additional teachers needed to accommodate these arrivals (rounded to the nearest ten) reflects the number needed to maintain baseline student-teacher ratios assuming that the enrolled population otherwise would have held steady.

concentrations of recent arrivals also may experience strain on their infrastructure, including school buildings, transportation, and technology.

Our county-level findings provide evidence of localized concentrations of this population of recent arrivals that the state estimates do not capture.[9] We estimate that newly arrived

---

[9] We note that our data sources do not permit us to estimate the full distribution of recently arrived children across the counties. Overall, we allocate about 72 percent of the children across the counties, with about 58 percent of the children allocated to the counties presented in Table A.4. The Migration Policy Institute data derived from the 2012–2016 American Community Survey we received were limited to the top 50 counties by total unauthorized immigrant population. The ORR data mask the counts for counties with fewer than 50 children placed with sponsors in a given fiscal year. See Appendix A for details.

undocumented and asylum-seeking children are at least 2 percent of the baseline student population for all but one of the top ten counties by number of recent arrivals (Dallas, Texas, being the exception), while recent arrivals do not exceed 2 percent of the baseline student population in any of the top ten states by number of recent arrivals. The largest percentage impacts among the top ten counties are in the counties surrounding Washington, D.C.: Prince George's County and Montgomery County, Maryland, and Fairfax County, Virginia. In six of the top ten counties, the recent arrivals represent at least 8 percent of the baseline Hispanic student population, whereas they are at least 8 percent of the baseline FRL student population in three of these counties (the three surrounding Washington, D.C., mentioned above). The recent arrivals are at least 3 percent of the baseline FRL population in all of the top ten counties except Dallas.

Overall, we estimate that Los Angeles County, California, and Harris County, Texas (which includes Houston), are the counties with the largest number of recently arrived undocumented and asylum-seeking children in this population enrolled in schools, accounting for more than 50,000 children (more than 15 percent of all such children) between them. These are also the only two counties for which we estimate that at least an additional 1,000 teachers would have been needed to maintain the baseline teacher-student ratios, assuming that their student populations otherwise would have held steady. However, because of the large size of these counties and the large existing Hispanic student populations, these counties did not experience one of the largest percentage impacts as a result of the recent wave of undocumented and asylum-seeking children.

Appendix A provides data for all 50 counties home to at least 1,000 recent arrivals, including estimates of counts and impacts relative to baseline populations of interest. We find that recently arrived undocumented and asylum-seeking children are more than 5 percent of the Hispanic student population at baseline in 14 counties not in the top ten in terms of the estimated number of these recent arrivals, including counties in California, Connecticut, Georgia, Louisiana, Maryland, Massachusetts, New Jersey, North Carolina, and Tennessee. While none of those 14 counties has more than 5,000 recent arrivals in its K–12 school systems, the large shares relative to the baseline population of Hispanic students could strain resources to a greater degree than areas with larger numbers of recent arrivals but with smaller relative impacts.

Summary and Implications for the Future

In sum, we estimate that about 575,000 children from Mexico and the Northern Triangle encountered CBP officials at the southwest border over the FYs 2017–2019 period. About 491,000 of them remained in the country in unresolved status as of March 2020, and about 321,000 of them were enrolled in K–12 schools at that time. Some states and counties are experiencing larger impacts from these recent arrivals than others, although it is likely that impacts are more locally concentrated than we are able to identify in the data. The impacts differ: In some locations, the newly arrived undocumented and asylum-seeking children represent a large share of the baseline student population, while in others they represent a large absolute number of students. California, Texas, Florida, New York, Virginia, Maryland, New Jersey, Georgia, North Carolina, and Louisiana account for about 75 percent of the recent arrivals. In four of those states—Virginia, Maryland, Georgia, and Louisiana—plus five more states and the District of Columbia, the recent arrivals represent more than 5 percent of the baseline Hispanic student population. To support the recent arrivals without changing teacher-student ratios, seven states would each have needed to hire at least 1,000 additional teachers and at least 1,000 additional other teaching staff. Los Angeles, California, and Harris County, Texas (which includes Houston), alone would need at least an additional 1,000 teachers to maintain the baseline teacher-student ratios.

Since FY 2019, the last year of arrivals we consider in our estimates, the COVID-19 pandemic has resulted in substantial impacts on both the flow of children to the Southwest border and U.S. policy toward these children. As discussed in Chapter One, border encounters in particular with children and family units fell precipitously at the outset of the pandemic in 2020, and then for a variety of reasons rebounded in early 2021. Meanwhile, Title 42 of the Public Health Safety Act (42 U.S.C. Chapter 6a) was used to turn migrants back on public health grounds, including children who might otherwise have been admitted into the country to pursue asylum. In tandem, these factors suggest that the number of recent arrivals entering the country and ultimately K–12 schools fell throughout much of 2020.

In the months and years ahead, the number of children arriving who enter U.S. schools will depend on both the flow of children to the border and policies toward those children. The limited variation in the share of children arriving over FYs 2017–2019 who remained in the country in unresolved status as of March 2020 suggests that—absent significant changes to how children and families are treated upon arrival, as occurred with the use of Title 42— the flow of arrivals will be the principal driver of the number of children in the country and in schools, as opposed to specific policies at the border. However, there is considerable uncertainty both with respect to how policy will evolve and whether the historically high levels of border encounters seen in early 2021 will persist.

Despite this uncertainty, local education policymakers seeking to accommodate recent arrivals could draw on our distributional estimates in tandem with real-time monthly data on border encounters to gain a sense of what to expect in their communities in the years to come. For example, if border encounters with unaccompanied children and families with children remain high throughout 2021 or beyond, and in particular should CBP cease using Title 42 to expel families (as it already has for unaccompanied children), states and counties where this population of children is concentrated could expect to see large numbers of future arrivals, including children, making their way through the system and from the border to communities around the country. Local planners could also draw on timely HHS data on states and counties where unaccompanied children are being placed with sponsors to manage expectations and gain an understanding of how the geographic distribution of arrivals may be changing over time.

CHAPTER THREE

The Federal and State Policy Landscapes

Having provided an estimate of the number and geographic distribution of undocumented and asylum-seeking children likely to be enrolled in K–12 schools, we now describe the federal policy context for the education of these children. We profile key dimensions of federal immigration law and policy in the past 30 years and then discuss the implications of these laws and policies for education. We then describe the role and efforts of the U.S. Department of Education to support the provision and quality of K–12 education, with emphasis on impediments to federal support. Lastly, we discuss the role of state and local education agencies (LEAs) in the education of undocumented and asylum-seeking children and discuss differences in practice and policy between states and districts and how these shape educational experiences.

How Federal Immigration Law and Policy Affect Migration of Children Over the U.S. Southwest Border

Federal immigration law and policy in the last 30 years have evolved to consolidate oversight of immigration, responding to ongoing debate that features two primary perspectives: a "rule-of-law" group, which asserts that immigration laws, as currently written, should be enforced, and a "humanitarian" group, which asserts that authorities must enforce laws in a matter that respects individual human rights, given the centrality of the belief in unalienable human rights to the founding of the nation (Ligor, 2018). In the past 30 years, congressional legislation, federal agency policy, and executive orders have largely stood on one side or the other of this divide, although they mostly lean more heavily toward rule-of-law approaches. Polarized immigration rhetoric has been counterproductive to meeting the goals of both groups (Nuñez-Neto, 2019). Although we will not exhaustively discuss federal laws and policies related to immigration in recent decades, we summarize some of the key actions and how they apply to the undocumented and asylum-seeking children that are the focus of our report. Table 3.1 lists immigration laws and policies from the past half century.

Federal immigration law in the 1990s reflected public concerns related to the rule of law, the perceived financial burden of immigrants on society, and the safety of communities; federal policy of this era aimed to reduce immigration numbers, remove immigrants who had committed crimes, and lower public benefit costs (Kohut, 2019). Legislation overhauled the

TABLE 3.1

Federal Immigration Policy and Target Populations

Year	Action	Immigrants	Nonimmigrants	Refugees/Asylees	Naturalized citizens	Noncitizens	Unauthorized Aliens
1962	Migration and Refugee Assistance Act of 1962			x			
1965	1965 Immigration and Nationality Act (Hart-Celler Act)	x					
1975	1975 Indochina Migration and Refugee Assistance Act			x			
1976	Immigration and Nationality Act Amendments of 1976	x					
1980	Refugee Act of 1980			x			
1986	Immigration Reform and Control Act (IRCA)						x
1988	Anti-Drug Abuse Act	x	x			x	x
1990	1990 Immigration Act	x	x			x	x
1994	Violent Crime Control and Law Enforcement Act (VCCLEA)	x	x			x	x
1996	Antiterrorism and Effective Death Penalty Act (AEDPA)	x	x			x	x
1996	Illegal Immigration Reform and Immigrant Responsibility Act (IIRIRA)	x	x	x		x	x
1997	Nicaraguan Adjustment and Central American Relief Act (NACARA)	x	x			x	x
1998	Haitian Refugee Immigration Fairness Act (HRIFA)	x	x			x	x
2001	USA Patriot Act	x	x			x	
2002	Enhanced Border Security and Visa Entry Reform Act	x	x	x		x	x
2002	Homeland Security Act	x	x	x		x	x
2005	REAL ID Act	x	x	x		x	x
2006	Secure Fence Act			x			x
2012	Deferred Action for Childhood Arrivals (DACA)						x
2014	Deferred Action for Parents of Americans and Lawful Permanent Residents (DAPA) and DACA Program Expanded						x
2017	DAPA program rescinded		x				x
2018	Family separations and family separations "for cause" only			x			x

SOURCES: Cohn, 2015; Migration Policy Institute, 2013; Pierce, 2019; Southern Poverty Law Center, 2020.

preference system that determines how visas are distributed among different groups, annual caps on immigration, and visa quotas; expanded the number and type of offenses warranting deportation of immigrants; and limited immigrants' admissibility and public benefits eligibility (Pub. L. 101-649, 1990; Pub. L. 104-193, 1996; Pub. L. 104-208, 1996).

After the September 11, 2001, attacks, the federal government acted to quell public anxiety about immigration, consolidating the oversight of immigration and scaling up enforcement. The Enhanced Border Security and Visa Entry Reform Act (Pub. L. 107-173, 2002) expanded the funding, staffing, and authority of immigration enforcement, and the Homeland Security Act (Pub. L. 107-296, 2002) created DHS, consolidating a patchwork of federal agencies and bureaus. The role of DHS in securing U.S. borders from entry of undocumented migrants has been codified through congressional (e.g., Secure Fence Act, Pub. L. 109-367, 2006), executive (e.g., Executive Order 13769, 2017; Executive Order 13780; 2017), and agency action (e.g., the rule finalization Inadmissibility on Public Charge Grounds [DHS, 2019c]) spanning nearly 20 years.

The U.S. government has also enacted several policies designed to combat human smuggling operations and address the causes of migration over the U.S. southwest border (Kamarck and Stenglein, 2019a). Efforts from the presidencies of George W. Bush to Donald Trump include the Dominican Republic-Central America Free Trade Agreement (CAFTA-DR), Millennium Challenge Corporation grants, and the Central American Regional Security Initiative, which together aimed to reduce migration over the U.S. southwest border. These efforts faced some criticism for not being effective enough, given ongoing arrivals. The U.S. and Northern Triangle governments have also engaged in public awareness campaigns to inform people about the potential dangers of undocumented migration and to correct possible misperceptions about U.S. immigration policies.

Although American lawmakers have marshaled substantial resources for the prevention and management of migration over the U.S. southwest border in recent decades, governmental action has largely failed to address the root causes of immigration or to stem the flow of immigrants, particularly from the Northern Triangle. Instead, federal immigration law and diplomatic efforts largely focus on deterrence of migration through efforts to secure the southern border and ports, as well punitive measures upon entry, in line with the rule-of-law camp.

The Trump administration focused its immigration-related efforts on border security. Among the most prominent U.S. policies during the Trump administration were the partial construction of a border wall and sending of active-duty troops to the border. These actions, while highly visible, likely did not have major impacts on migration, as 2019 saw peaks of migration not seen in over a decade, as described in Chapter One.

In January 2019, DHS began implementing the MPP, also known as "Remain in Mexico." Under the MPP, certain people attempting to enter the United States illegally or without documentation, including those who claim asylum, were no longer to be released into the United States while awaiting adjudication of their status. Instead, these people were given a "notice to appear" for their immigration court hearing and would be returned to Mexico until their hearing date. DHS explained that this action was taken in reaction to the increase in arrivals of family units, which overwhelmed the U.S. immigration system. According to DHS, misguided court decisions and outdated laws have also made it easier for such migrants to enter and remain in the United States if they are adults who arrive with children, unaccompanied children, or individuals who fraudulently claim asylum (DHS, 2019a). In February 2021, DHS began processing individuals in Mexico with active MPP cases (DHS, 2021). However, this policy has affected only a small proportion of arrivals. An estimated 60,000 arrivals have gone through this system, representing just over 7 percent of apprehensions in the most recent fiscal year (American Immigration Council, 2020).

Additional deterrence policies the United States has pursued include family separation, narrowed eligibility grounds for asylum, restrictions on the number of asylum seekers allowed into ports of entry each day, and limitations on the right of asylum seekers to work legally. Northern Triangle agreements are a new measure by which migrants from Honduras and El Salvador who seek protections at the U.S. southern border will be asked whether they sought protections in Guatemala first. If they did not, they are to be sent back to Guatemala (Nuñez-Neto, 2019).

The Biden administration has faced significant increases in migration across the U.S. southwest border in its early months. During the first 100 days of the administration, monthly border crossings reached a 15-year high as of March 2021 (Hackman, 2021). There has been an increase in unaccompanied children, families with young children, and single men coming to the border. The winter 2021 surge in migrants at the southern border led President Biden to elevate this issue as a key foreign policy issue, putting Vice President Kamala Harris in charge of finding solutions, negotiating with Central American governments, and making public statements to discourage migrants. The Biden administration has continued to enforce Title 42 of the Public Health Safety Act (42 U.S.C. Chapter 6a), a Trump-era public health policy that allows migrants to be turned back without entry or the opportunity to seek asylum in the interest of mitigating the spread of COVID-19 but has lifted the pandemic-induced moratorium on green card issuance begun in spring 2020 (Watson, 2021). The Biden administration is concurrently working to pass legislation and enact policies that align more with the "humanitarian" immigration debate position, with proposals to significantly raise the annual cap on refugees, continue the DACA program, and stop enforcement of Trump-era restrictions on green card issuance for individuals who have used or are at risk of using public benefits (Krogstad and Gonzalez-Barrera, 2021).

What Happens to Migrant Children at the Border?

Migrant children who arrive to the southwest border can take several paths through the U.S. immigration system, depending on country of origin and whether they arrived unaccompanied or with a parent or guardian. This involves interaction with and handoffs among multiple federal agencies. Here we describe the experiences, first, of unaccompanied children and, second, of children arriving with families.

Unaccompanied Children

CBP officials who encounter an unaccompanied child at the border must first determine whether the child meets the statutory definition of *unaccompanied*: under 18, lacking legal status, and "without a parent or legal guardian in the United States who is available to provide care and physical custody" (Kandel, 2019). Unaccompanied children from all countries may pursue asylum claims, with U.S. Citizenship and Immigration Services taking the lead in adjudicating those claims. What happens after a child meets CBP officials depends on a child's country of origin.

Unaccompanied children from noncontiguous countries (e.g., the Northern Triangle countries) must be transferred from CBP custody by U.S. Immigration and Customs Enforcement (ICE) to the HHS ORR facilities within 72 hours. In reality, many children have stayed in CBP holding facilities longer than the mandated 72 hours—particularly more recently—because of lack of space in ORR shelters, leading CBP to open additional shelters for children (Gramlich, 2021). From CBP facilities, children are placed in standard removal proceedings before the DOJ EOIR. ORR is responsible for children's custody, care, and education, as well as for identifying a suitable sponsor to whom they are released while their EOIR cases are in process. In FY 2019, unaccompanied children were in ORR care for an average of about two months (ORR, 2021). Once a child is placed in the custody of a sponsor, they have access to education in the public school served by the sponsor's state and district of residence.

Unaccompanied children from Mexico or Canada (contiguous countries) must be screened by CBP officials within 48 hours to determine whether they are victims of human trafficking, have a credible fear of returning to their home country, or are unable to decide on their own whether or not to return. If none of those hold, these children "must" return home voluntarily, although they can do so without suffering any consequences (Kandel, 2019).

The complex policy environment described above creates a network of federal and local agencies that have responsibility for unaccompanied migrant children at different points in time. The U.S. Department of Education, which may seem to be the natural choice for ensuring the provision and quality of immigrant children's education, in actuality has limited purview due to the legal status and responsibility of other federal agencies. Our interviewees noted that it is not always clear in practice who is responsible for ensuring that immigrant children have access to education, and this may contribute to gaps in educational access. Below are the entities responsible at various points:

- *At apprehension/in detention: DHS and, specifically, CBP.* When children are apprehended by border patrol officers and it is determined that they are unaccompanied, they are transferred to the care and custody of HHS ORR within 72 hours. There are no requirements for educational provision while children are in the custody of DHS.

- *In temporary shelters: HHS ORR.* HHS is required by law to care for unaccompanied children apprehended while crossing the U.S. border. While children are in the care of HHS shelters, they receive educational services and other care from providers who run the shelters. They are not enrolled in public schools. Educational provision while in ORR custody operates independent of the public education system. Consequently, curricula are unaligned, and children's educational records might not be complete or transferrable.

- *Settled with sponsors in community: ORR and an LEA* (U.S. Department of Education, 2014b). When children are released from federal custody to a sponsor, the responsibility for their education shifts to local educational agencies, although verification of the receipt of education remains the responsibility of ORR, which is within HHS. While children reside with a sponsor, they have a right to a public education in their local communities. ORR is responsible for verifying school enrollment with sponsors. The transition from ORR custody to the custody of sponsors may lead to gaps in educational provision due to inconsistent access to education records from ORR custody, difficulty meeting the enrollment requirements of LEAs, and lack of oversight by ORR.

Figure 3.1 illustrates the process between the border and school for unaccompanied children.

FIGURE 3.1

The Process Between the Border and School for Unaccompanied Children

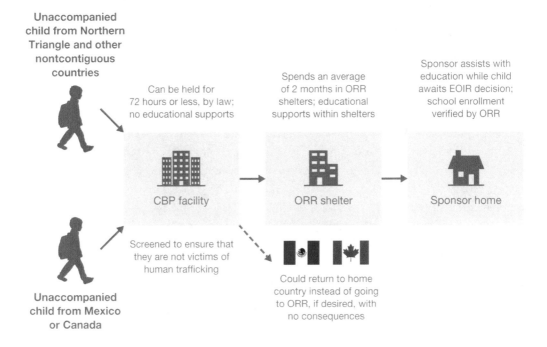

Children Arriving with Families

Administrative processing for children who arrive with a parent or legal guardian also begins with their CBP encounter. From there, some families enter standard removal proceedings before EOIR, while others are processed for *expedited removal* (a streamlined process with limited due-process rights) (Smith, 2019) unless they claim and are determined by U.S. Citizenship and Immigration Services to have a credible or reasonable fear of returning to their country of origin. While their EOIR cases are in process, these children may be held in family detention centers maintained by ICE or released along with their families. In general, courts have ruled that children may be held in detention for no more than 20 days and have favored keeping families together (Peck and Harrington, 2018). Figure 3.2 illustrates this process.

In 2018, DOJ implemented a "zero tolerance" policy that criminally prosecuted illegal border crossers, including parents traveling with children and seeking asylum. This resulted in family separations because the parents were held in DOJ facilities where children are not permitted, while the children were treated as *unaccompanied* on the grounds that they did not have an available caretaker. About 3,000 children were separated from their families under this policy, with "thousands more" were possibly separated prior to its formal announcement (Kandel, 2021). Although the policy is no longer active, an estimated 545 children remain separated from their parents (Dickerson, 2021).

FIGURE 3.2

The Process Between the Border and School for Children in Family Units

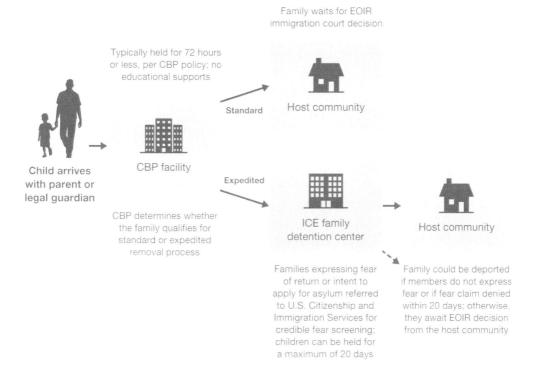

What Is Federal Policy Regarding Access to Education for Undocumented and Asylum-Seeking Children?

The U.S. Constitution guarantees equal educational opportunity for all children in the United States, regardless of citizenship or immigration status. This means that all children in the United States have a right to a free public education. This right is codified in the Bill of Rights and reaffirmed in Titles IV and VI of the Civil Rights Act of 1964 (Pub. L. 88-352, 1964). The Civil Rights Act bans discrimination "on the basis of race, color, or national origin" in "programs and activities receiving federal financial assistance" (DOJ, undated). However, a lack of specificity about education within these laws for undocumented children within federal legislation—and the predominance of rule-of-law policy legislative approaches over the past 30 years—has led to Supreme Court cases establishing the educational rights of immigrant children.

Supreme Court rulings have established that children have a right to education regardless of immigration status, set requirements regarding the provision of education while in federal custody, and clarified constitutional educational practices for children with limited English proficiency (see the "Key Policies Supporting Access to Education for Newcomer Immigrant Children and Youth" box). In response to a September 1977 class action lawsuit filed in Texas "on behalf of certain school-age children of Mexican origin residing in Smith County, who could not establish that they had been legally admitted into the United States," the Supreme Court's 5–4 1982 decision in *Plyler v. Doe* (1982) extended the interpretation of the 14th Amendment's Equal Protection Clause to apply to anyone who lives in the United States. According to *Plyler v. Doe*, children "can affect neither their parents' conduct nor their own status" and should therefore be entitled to the education that "has a fundamental role in maintaining the fabric of our society." In alignment with the ruling, undocumented children residing in the United States are to be afforded the same rights and opportunities to participate in the public education system as U.S. citizens and other legal residents (National Association of Secondary School Principals, undated). The ruling stipulates a set of restrictions for public schools (Washington Office of Superintendent of Public Instruction, 2017), which shall not deny admission to students based on undocumented status or require students or parents to disclose or document their immigration status. As an extension of these requirements, administrators and personnel are also not legally required to enforce U.S. immigration laws, and districts are discouraged from requesting Social Security numbers from students or family members in documentation, such as for enrollment or applications for National School Lunch Program low-cost or free meals and other support programs.

Another Supreme Court Ruling, *Reno v. Flores* (1993), led to the *Flores* Settlement Agreement in 1997. The agreement represents the federal response to a decade-long campaign against "mistreatment of alien minors in detention facilities." Prior to *Flores*, children were legally not to be released to anyone other than a close relative. But ongoing concerns about detention conditions led to the 1997 agreement requiring the government to release children "without necessary delay" to a broader list of designated individuals, placement of children

Key Policies Supporting Access to Education for Newcomer Immigrant Children and Youth

- U.S. Bill of Rights and Civil Rights Act of 1964 (Pub. L. 88-352, 1964): All children in the United States are guaranteed equal access to educational opportunity, regardless of citizenship and immigration status.
- *Lau v. Nichols* (1974): This Supreme Court ruling required supplemental language instruction for students with limited English proficiency (see U.S. Department of Health, Education and Welfare, 1975).
- Lau Remedies (1975): The U.S. Department of Health, Education, and Welfare issued pedagogical guidelines for schools to promote the provision of an equal education for non-English-speaking students.
- *Plyler v. Doe* (1982): This Supreme Court ruling reaffirmed that school-age children are entitled to education, regardless of the immigration status of their parents.
- *Reno v. Flores* (1993): This Supreme Court ruling required that unaccompanied children cannot be detained by CBP for longer than 20 days, which has educational implications given that CBP does not provide educational supports.
- *Flores* Settlement Agreement (1997): This federal response to the *Reno v. Flores* decision provided for the release of detained undocumented children "without necessary delay" to a broader list of designated individuals and also created and implemented of standards of care for immigrant children in detention (see Sussis, 2019).
- DACA (2012): This executive action provided protection from deportation for individuals brought to the United States as minor children who have lived in the United States since 2007 (Napolitano, 2012).

in the "least restrictive" appropriate setting, and the creation and implementation of standards of care for immigrant children in detention (Sussis, 2019). The current interpretation of *Flores* requires "unaccompanied alien children" and any other detained child to be released within 20 days, and the issue remains significant in discussions of family separations at the southwest border and the provision of quality education while in federal custody and after release (Sussis, 2019).

The Supreme Court has also made rulings that have guided the educational practices for children who are learning English. In 1974, the Court made a unanimous decision in *Lau v. Nichols* (1974) that Title VI of the Civil Rights Act of 1964 requires equal treatment for students with limited English proficiency and ruled that districts must make affirmative remedial efforts to ensure a "meaningful education" for all students. The following year, the U.S. Department of Health, Education, and Welfare issued the Lau Remedies, a set of pedagogical guidelines for schools to promote an equal education for non-English-speaking students. The Lau Remedies directed school districts to identify, evaluate, and provide transitional bilingual instruction for students with limited English proficiencies. The enforcement of the Lau Remedies, and of the subsequent notice of proposed rulemaking in the *Federal Register* by the

Department of Education in 1980, promoted growth in supplemental and bilingual instruction for children across the country (DOJ, 2000; Malakoff and Hakuta, 1990).

The federal actions regarding this population that might have received the most media attention in recent years were the Obama administration executive memoranda providing protections for unauthorized immigrant children and adults. DACA was announced in 2012 and provided protection from deportation and temporary work authorization to individuals who were brought to the United States as minor children and had lived in the United States since June 15, 2007 (Napolitano, 2012). The 2014 DAPA memorandum deferred deportation and provided other protections for unauthorized immigrants whose children are American citizens or lawful permanent residents (Johnson, 2014). These executive memoranda were intended to increase stability and opportunity for children brought into the country as minors without documentation or born in the United States since their parents' unauthorized arrival. Early evidence suggests that these memoranda have contributed to positive outcomes for children and families. There is growing evidence that DACA contributed to increased rates of high school attendance and graduation and improved the physical and mental health of eligible noncitizen immigrants (Hainmueller et al., 2017; Kuka, Shenhav, and Shih, 2020; Patler and Pirtle, 2018). Although the temporary work authorization provision may increase economic stability and community integration of DACA recipients and their families (Gonzales, Terriquez, and Ruszczyk, 2014), it may also reduce investment in higher education by increasing the opportunity cost of educational investment (Hsin and Ortega, 2018).

What State Immigration Policies Shape Access to Education for Undocumented and Asylum-Seeking Children?

Following federal law, states and LEAs are charged with the provision of a public education for all children living within the state. State policies related to immigration and education shape undocumented and asylum-seeking children's access to public education, as well as the quality of that education.

State immigration law can affect the educational experiences of undocumented and asylum-seeking children living in those states by shaping their interactions with public organizations—specifically, K–12 schools. State policy action in this area has generally represented either a reiteration of or compensatory reaction against federal policy. For example, in 2020, the exclusion of undocumented immigrants and individuals and children in mixed-status families from the Coronavirus Aid, Relief, and Economic Security (CARES) Act stimulus package prompted several states to authorize new state funding and community outreach to immigrant communities (Suro and Findling, 2020; Pub. L. 116-136, 2020). Examples of state resistance to federal directives related to immigration can be found in Obama-era state challenges brought against the 2014 Department of Homeland Security memorandum that established DAPA and Trump-era state action barring state personnel and resources from being used to cooperate or share information with federal ICE officials (Dinan, 2020). Immigration policy adopted in one state may diffuse to other states. Arizona's Senate Bill 1070, which added new requirements and penalties related to the enforcement of immigration law to mitigate the possibility of restriction of enforcement, was followed by the introduction of similar bills in at least half a dozen other states (Morse, 2011).

What Are Federal and State Resources and Responsibilities Regarding the Education of Undocumented and Asylum-Seeking Children?

Although the federal role in education has expanded since the mid-20th century, education remains primarily a state and local responsibility. SEAs are responsible for administering federal and state education laws, dispersing federal and state financial resources, and providing guidance and support for LEAs or school districts. In this section, we discuss the resources and responsibilities of both the federal and state departments of education for the education of undocumented and asylum-seeking children.

Federal Resources and Responsibilities

The U.S. Department of Education provides two major resources for the education of children: (1) It administers formula grant programs, and (2) it develops materials and convenes professionals to support states and districts in meeting federal requirements for educational provision. Efforts within these domains to support the population we study are focused on the development of English proficiency and mitigation of the negative impacts of educational disruption. The U.S. Department of Education provides financial resources and guidance in the form of fact sheets, tool kits, and networks for state agency staff to "help educational leaders better understand the responsibilities of States and local educational agencies" to educate new immigrant students (U.S. Department of Education, 2014a).

Key U.S. Department of Education Programs Supporting Schools as They Provide Education for Newcomer Immigrant Children and Youth

- **Title I, Part A, Elementary and Secondary Education Act** (Pub. L. 89-10, 1965) provides funding for disadvantaged populations, which may include immigrant students.
- **Title III, Elementary and Secondary Education Act,** provides formula grants to SEAs, which are then provided to LEAs to support the education of English learners, including instruction, family engagement, and professional development, as well as other activities to improve outcomes for ELLs.

The federal government provides programming and resources through the title programs established by the Elementary and Secondary Education Act (Pub. L. 89-10, 1965); the aim of the act and its subsequent reauthorizations is to provide equitable access to education for all children. The 2015 Every Student Succeeds Act (ESSA), a reauthorization of the Elementary and Secondary Education Act (Pub. L. 114-95, 2015) signed during the Obama administration, authorizes more than $24.5 billion in funding to be distributed across multiple programs. The formula grant programs of note for the support of the education of this population of children are Title I (Parts A and C) and Title III:

- **Title I** is the largest Elementary and Secondary Education Act allocation, constituting roughly 20 percent of the annual federal education budget. Title I funds programs intended to promote access to quality education for disadvantaged students; it indirectly supports the students in our study by providing school funding intended to address disadvantages across a range of populations. Part A, for the "economically and socially disadvantaged" is the most applicable to our population of study.
  - **Part A** provides formula grants to LEAs and to specific schools within LEAs with high numbers or percentages of children from low-income families.
- **Title III** supports quality education, language instruction, and supplemental services for ELL students by developing and sustaining programs related to English proficiency, professional development for school staff, and activities to promote community engagement (Thornley, 2017). SEAs receive Title III funding; SEAs use a small portion of the grant for state-level activities and direct the remaining funds to LEAs, typically based on a per pupil count of the number of identified ELLs attending school within the LEA. Depending on how SEAs elect to structure their subgrants, LEAs with significant growth in the number of immigrant students in their populations may be eligible for additional funding under Title III provisions (California Department of Education, 2020a). Title III has been a key tool to address the needs of districts serving newcomer students; it invests additional funding and encourages states to delineate set-aside funds for districts serving immigrant students, to be supplemented by federal grant funding.

Although not specifically targeted to immigrant children or language development, Title IV is another potential source of resources to bolster the education of immigrant children. Title IV Part A, the Student Support and Academic Enrichment Program, provides resources to increase the capacity of educational organizations to serve their students. Title IV, Part A, allows for support to provide a well-rounded education, improve school conditions, and improve the use of technology (Pub. L. 114-95, 2015).

The U.S. Department of Education also produces guidance materials and connects professionals to assist school administrators in navigating the complex policy landscape. These materials are developed and published by the pertinent offices within the Department of Education, including the Office of Civil Rights, Office of English Language Acquisition (OELA), and National Clearinghouse of English Language Acquisition, and include manuals, tool kits,

"Dear Colleague" letters, and analyses. For instance, in May 2014, DOJ and the Department of Education published a letter with guidance directing SEAs and LEAs to assess documents requested for enrollment to ensure that procedures did not have a chilling effect on students' abilities to access education and to review enrollment data for signals that may indicate barriers to attendance (Lhamon, Rosenfelt, and Samuels, 2014). Another letter in October 2015 accompanied a resource guide and tool kit to assist SEA and LEA administrators in serving undocumented children, with a specific emphasis on supporting DACA students (U.S. Department of Education, 2017a). The resources, accessible on the Department of Education's website, highlight a number of guides, guidance letters, and other tool kits to promote SEA and LEA engagement with immigrant children populations (U.S. Department of Education, 2017b). Links to the 2014 DOJ and Department of Education guidance letter, a fact sheet, and a question-and-answer document support the implementation of considerations under *Plyler v. Doe* for K–12 students.

Additional HHS ORR services to assist SEAs and LEAs in supporting education for undocumented and asylum-seeking children include the "New Immigrant Guide" (meant for all immigrant children, not only the children in our study) published by U.S. Citizenship and Immigration Services (2015) and a catalog of fact sheets offered by the Department of Education's Office of English Language Acquisition (2020). Educational resources for DACA students are also listed, presenting general information, frequently asked questions about education records, and a tool kit for collaborative action between students, parents, and community partners. The Department of Education also provides technical support by undertaking and disseminating analysis: The Office of English Language Acquisition (2018) and the National Clearinghouse of English Language Acquisition (undated) analyze and report on national snapshots of graduation rates, growth in the number of ELLs and newcomers. States can request reports for their state, with information about students and programs.

The Department of Education also seeks to build the capacity of SEAs by connecting staff within a program. For instance, the Migrant Education Program (MEP; Title I, Part C, of the Elementary and Secondary Education Act) has the MEP Coordination Work Group (Migrant Education Program, undated). The MEP Coordination Work Group brings SEA staff together to build capacity, discuss common challenges, and share promising practices.

The U.S. Department of Education also supports the education of immigrant children by coordinating with foreign governments to facilitate the transfer of educational records and bolster educational opportunity. For instance, through a formalized memorandum of understanding, the U.S. Department of Education and the Mexican Secretariat of Public Education exchange information and records, which supports more-seamless enrollment and appropriate placement of newcomers to the United States from Mexico (International Affairs Office, 2015; Villalobos and Duncan, 2018).

Obstacles to Local Education Agencies Receiving Available Federal Support

According to our interviews with stakeholders, the chief impediments to federal support for undocumented and asylum-seeking children were understanding of the law, navigating the policy context, and receiving adequate funding.

Limited Understanding at the School Level of Requirements for the Education of Undocumented and Asylum-Seeking Children

Stakeholders pointed to a lack of understanding among staff in schools about federal requirements for providing quality education to undocumented and asylum-seeking children. When expressing concerns about appropriate educational provision, participants cited unknowing or willful failure to enroll or adequately educate these students as an ongoing concern. For example, state and federal interview participants suggested that much of the concern lies with the interpretation of policy and day-to-day practices of school district employees, particularly those who interact with families of undocumented and asylum-seeking children seeking to enroll their children or receive other services. For instance, a secretary in the district office may mistakenly tell a family that a Social Security number is required for enrollment even though children can be enrolled without one. To mitigate lack of understanding or willful action, federal and state agencies serve as resources for questions and disseminators of key information. For example, the Office of Bilingual Education and World Languages in the New York State Education Department designs and disseminates resources, including questionnaires for oral interviews, screeners for multilingual literacy and writing skills, and an identification flow chart, among other resources, to support districts and schools in the education of students with interrupted formal education (New York State Education Department, 2021). The U.S. Department of Education, particularly the Office of Civil Rights, fields questions, creates and disseminates clarifying materials, and connects state and district staff to resources and information. Through these actions, the department resolves misunderstandings and holds states and districts accountable for their support of all children.

A Complex Policy Ecosystem Involving Many Agencies at Different Levels of Government

The policy ecosystem surrounding the legal status and educational experience of undocumented and asylum-seeking children is an impediment to the education of this population. Immigration law has created a patchwork of guidance and requirements that leave minors with various points of contact for different facets of their lives, education, and well-being in the United States. The implications of the complexity of immigration law were particularly salient for interviewed stakeholders when considering the various federal agencies that bear some responsibility for the well-being and education of the population of interest but might not communicate with one another. Furthermore, federal agencies typically do not communicate adequately with SEAs and LEAs about the populations they have served before they pass them off to sponsors or others. Although federal law guarantees minors' right to an education, and U.S. Department of Education grant programs are intended to ensure that states and districts have adequate resources to serve these students, the laws and programs often breed misunderstanding for students, families, and educational staff alike, and policy leaves gaps in support of the needs of students beyond their academic enrichment. Stakeholders expressed concern that continued lack of attention to the "upstream" problems in the immigration system will continue to yield "downstream" challenges in the U.S. education system.

Federal Dollars Could Be Diverted from the Target Population

Stakeholders also expressed concerns regarding the flow of financial resources intended for the education of undocumented and asylum-seeking children. The Elementary and Secondary Education Act title programs should ultimately direct dollars to the support of academic enrichment of students. Some congressional staff expressed concerns that allocated funds do not ultimately end up directly targeted for the support of education and services for undocumented and asylum-seeking children but rather get diverted to shore up funding needed to support general programs and expenses for all children.

State Resources and Responsibilities

SEAs are responsible for supporting and monitoring the legality of policies and practices at local school districts. There are many dimensions to the ongoing monitoring and operation of schools for which SEAs are responsible. For example, SEAs are expected to monitor district adherence to the federal requirement that undocumented and asylum-seeking children have a right to an education, ensure that districts obey state education law regarding student eligibility for enrollment and instructional practices, collect data and create systems for holding districts accountable for the academic progress their students make, and license and verify the qualification of teachers.

SEAs also play a key role in facilitating access to and the administration of federal grant programs for the support of undocumented and asylum-seeking children. Depending on the program, federal grants either are administered by the U.S. Department of Education but flow through the SEA or are administered by the SEA, which is responsible for making and monitoring subgrants to LEAs. In either case, SEAs are responsible for monitoring the needs of students and the demands on districts resulting from shifts in student needs. SEAs collect data from LEAs regarding their student population and student progress, analyze these data, and report up to the U.S. Department of Education. Additionally, SEAs leverage this information to identify needs and justify federal grant applications.

Like the U.S. Department of Education, SEAs also provide guidance for districts, develop and distribute informational materials on complex policy areas or thorny problems of practice, and provide training for district staff. Most SEAs have divisions that are responsible for administering each of the federal title programs and that oversee the education and welfare of key student groups. For instance, ELL directors or coordinators support the district-level supervisors of ELL programs and their teaching staffs. SEAs might provide guidance regarding problems of practice and the teacher certification process, organize conferences for relevant staff around the state, and draft reports and tool kits for use by district-level ELL staff. SEAs also provide training for district staff to ensure that LEAs and families have correct and detailed information to support access to and the provision of quality education.

Key Differences in How States Support Undocumented and Asylum-Seeking Children

Earlier in this chapter, we summarized various ways in which state immigration policies can support undocumented and asylum-seeking children. Here, we discuss the state role in schooling of undocumented and asylum-seeking children. States are responsible for the oversight of laws and guidelines surrounding the establishment and management of public education. These laws often pertain to enhanced learning for refugees or ELLs in K–12 education or immigration and residency requirements for access to in-state tuition or financial assistance at colleges and universities (Morse et al., 2016; Morse, Pimienta, and Chanda, 2018; Morse, 2019; Morse, 2020; Morse, 2021; Serna, Cohen, and Nguyen, 2017; Mendoza and Shaikh, 2019). State statutes regarding K–12 education can provide guidelines and funding for resources that shape the quality of education for students. In 2020, Colorado House Bill 1001a (Grants to Improve Internet Access in P–12 Education) allocated resources to help students, educators, and other LEA staff access broadband internet to reduce the risk of learning loss for vulnerable populations during COVID-19 (Morse, 2021), an important resource for education that may be particularly scarce for the population of interest (Cherewka, 2020). Also in 2020, California Senate Bill 115 (Budget Act) allocated funding for childcare and legal services for unaccompanied undocumented children (Morse, 2021). State statutes can also change the landscape of K–12 educational credentials to better recognize the unique and substantial achievements of ELLs (Morse, 2021). For example, in 2016, Arizona Senate Bill 1239 established a "state seal of biliteracy for students who graduate with a high level of proficiency in one or more languages in addition to English" to recognize the accomplishment of students who demonstrate proficiency in one or more languages other than English and identify this accomplishment for employers and postsecondary institutions (Morse et al., 2016).

Consequently, there is variation from state to state in laws that shape the experiences of undocumented and asylum-seeking children, as discussed above. We list some of the key differences below. In addition, given our case studies in Louisiana and California school districts (discussed in the next chapter), we also unpack some key policy differences in those specific states in the "Training and Guidance for Supporting English Language Learners by Louisiana and California State Education Agencies" box.

Guidance and Opportunities for Enrollment of Older Teenagers

For students with interrupted or limited formal education, one facet of education law that heavily shapes their experience is public school attendance age limits. The maximum age at which students are able to attend varies by state (Diffey and Steffes, 2017). Some states have strict upper age limits for public school attendance, usually between 19 and 22 years old, while others do not have statute guiding the upper age limit and leave discretion to LEAs (five

Training and Guidance for Supporting English Language Learners by Louisiana and California State Education Agencies

According to our interviewees, the Louisiana Department of Education holds varied, targeted trainings for district staff:

- During semiannual trainings with school district title program directors, Department of Education staff disseminate information that district staff need to carry out their responsibilities under federal grant programs.
- The SEA also arranges professional development sessions facilitated by legal experts, often in collaboration with the Southern Poverty Law Center, related to civil rights, equal opportunity laws, and other relevant topics. These noncompulsory sessions are well attended by district faculty and staff.
- Other trainings are focused on dispelling misinformation among LEA staff and developing strategies for establishing reliable information networks and building trust with the undocumented and asylum-seeking community.

According to our interviewees, the California Department of Education targets professional development support to districts with substantial need and develops informational resources for broad use across the state:

- The Bilingual Coordinators Network supports district bilingual education coordinators by providing shared professional development and networking opportunities for the 15 districts with the most ELLs (California Department of Education, 2021). This forum allows the SEA to disseminate ESSA Title III program information and build a community for members to discuss current and relevant research, disseminate information on student needs and supports, and collaborate on policy work.
- The California English Learner Roadmap provides guidance on ELL pathways and relevant policy considerations and illuminates concepts with case studies; the project defines principles to align practices, services, relationships, and approaches to teaching and learning across the California educational system (California Department of Education, 2020b).

states and the District of Columbia; Diffey and Steffes, 2017). Statutes that enforce an upper age limit for public schooling have implications for who is served by the public school system. Undocumented and asylum-seeking children who enter the U.S. school system with limited or interrupted formal education may be unable to graduate by the age of 18, so statutes on upper age limits may shape both legal access to public education and the guidance from educators regarding coursework and pathways through high school.

Public Benefits Eligibility and Other Forms of State Aid for Undocumented and Asylum-Seeking Children and Families

It may be more or less difficult to retain undocumented and asylum-seeking teenagers in school depending on other supports and resources for which children and families may be eligible. One SEA stakeholder drew on experience working with ELLs in a number of different states and noted that public supports for children and families contribute to better persistence and performance in school, as teenagers do not feel pressure to leave school and go to work to contribute. In addition, families may be able to better oversee and support the education of their children if they are receiving such supports.

Eligibility for In-State Tuition and Financial Aid

Undocumented children are not eligible for federal financial aid, so state tuition policies and aid eligibility are important factors that shape the accessibility of postsecondary training for undocumented and asylum-seeking children. Aid eligibility for undocumented students leads to greater college enrollment for Hispanic students, increases in credits attempted and completed, and higher rates of college persistence and graduation (Ngo and Astudillo, 2019). Stakeholders at school districts and community organizations noted the role of state tuition and financial aid policy in encouraging or discouraging aspirations and efforts to earn postsecondary credentials among undocumented children and young adults.

States have taken different approaches to policies regarding access to in-state tuition and state financial assistance for postsecondary education. The affordability of college is a major factor in student access to learning beyond high school, and the provision of grant aid increases the probability of enrollment, persistence, and attainment of a postsecondary degree or credential (Nguyen, Kramer, and Evans, 2019). Students who are not U.S. citizens are ineligible for federal financial aid, and in the majority of states, residents who are not U.S. citizens are not eligible for in-state tuition rates or state-administered financial aid. Seventeen states and the District of Columbia presently offer in-state tuition benefits for in-state high school graduates who have been accepted to state colleges or universities (Morse, 2021). At least 11 states, seven state university systems, and a number of individual state colleges and universities have enacted legislation or established policies to allow undocumented students to be eligible for state financial aid (Morse, 2021). Several states have taken a different approach: Six states prohibit undocumented students from receiving in-state tuition benefits.

Teacher Labor Markets and Regulation of Teaching Qualifications

The local labor market, opportunities for further training, and the degree of stringency or leniency regarding certification and licensure all have implications for the staffing and quality of educational instruction for undocumented and asylum-seeking children. Stakeholders at the state and district levels noted that there are critical staffing needs, particularly for staff who have language proficiency aligned with the local migrant communities. Unfortunately, labor markets might not have many individuals with the requisite certifications who also have these language skills; regulations regarding certification serve as a barrier to hiring individuals who have the language skill sets and interest but lack the formal education or certification needed to qualify for vacant roles.

Local Differences in Education Policy and Practice

Local districts maintain authority for school enrollment and the implementation of public schooling. Consequently, some differences in policy and practice at the local level contribute to differences in the educational experiences of undocumented and asylum-seeking children. Our policy informants provided thoughts about key variation in how LEAs support these children, which are summarized here. However, the next chapter provides much more detail on potential differences, drawing on interviews with numerous school system staff in our case study schools.

Documentation for Enrollment

School districts are permitted to require students or their parents to provide proof of residency within the district (per *Martinez v. Bynum*, 1983). For example, a school district may require copies of lease agreements or utility bills to establish the residency of children. There is variation among districts as to what documents they require to establish residency. However, in accordance with federal law and U.S. Department of Education guidance (Lhamon, Rosenfelt, and Samuels, 2014), districts must ensure that required documents do not "unlawfully bar or discourage" the enrollment or attendance of undocumented children or children whose parents are undocumented.

Administrative Burden for Children and Families

Although federal law defines the right of children to an education, front-line staff in districts may create administrative burden for children and families through unwitting or willful complication of enrollment and ongoing administrative processes. Federal policymakers and federal and state agency staff reported confusion from districts regarding federal and state policy surrounding documentation and age and school enrollment, as well as variation in the processes that districts adopt for enrollment and other administrative processes.

Overall, although federal protections and programs are in place alongside state administrative support and additional guidance, dissemination of information and adherence to the law remain challenges.

Summary

Minors entering the United States encounter a complex policy ecosystem that shapes their transition to U.S. life and educational experience. Immigration law has shaped the makeup and timing of entering newcomers and created a patchwork of guidance and requirements that leave minors with various points of contact for different facets of their lives, education, and well-being. Federal law guarantees minors' right to an education, and federal programs administered by the U.S. Department of Education (through SEAs and LEAs) are intended to provide the necessary resources for LEAs to support newcomers' development of English proficiency and mitigate the negative academic impacts of disrupted education, but those laws and programs are typically not designed to address anything beyond the academic needs of newcomers. Differences in state and LEA policies likely have more impact on the educational experiences of newcomer minors than do federal policies.

CHAPTER FOUR

Educator Experiences in California and Louisiana

In this chapter, we move from looking at trends in policies to focusing on the experiences of administrators and educators who serve the educational needs of students in two very different contexts: a school district in Louisiana that has recently experienced large increases in the population of newcomer children and a school district in California that has been serving large numbers of these children for many years.

We often use the terms *newcomers* and *ELLs* as shorthand in this chapter, instead of *undocumented and asylum-seeking children*, since these are often the terms that the educators we spoke with used in our discussions, given that they often do not know the immigration status of their students. In particular, we can comment only on the numbers of ELLs served by schools, because those numbers are documented by school systems, whereas the numbers of undocumented and asylum-seeking students are not documented by schools in any formal way. Some of the issues, challenges, and strategies we discuss in this chapter are ones intended to support all newcomer or ELLs, but we discuss them because they also provide important supports to undocumented and asylum-seeking children.

We start by briefly discussing the state context for education of undocumented and asylum-seeking children in each of the school districts and provide an overview of the services available to the students in our study in both of the school districts. We then go into some detail on the successes and challenges that administrators and educators perceive in supporting undocumented and asylum-seeking students in two school districts, including challenges related to enrollment, English learning and academics, nonacademic needs, and teacher training. Lastly, we summarize a few key policy challenges that our district informants raised that are also relevant to what they are able to do and offer in their districts.

Readers should keep in mind that our findings in this chapter are necessarily limited by our very small case study sample and the interviewees with whom we spoke for our case studies. Nonetheless, these findings offer an on-the-ground, more detailed perspective on the useful approaches and challenges related to supporting undocumented and asylum-seeking children who enter school systems.

State Policy Context for Supporting Undocumented and Asylum-Seeking Children in Louisiana and California

Louisiana and California differ in terms of the total number of immigrant children being served in each state's K–12 schools. According to Kids Count data (Annie E. Casey Foundation, 2021), as of 2019, California was home to 112,000 children under the age of 18 with parents who had been in the country five years or less, which accounted for 3 percent of California's total child population, whereas Louisiana was home to about 2,000 such children, or 2 percent of its total child population. Kids Count data likely undercount total numbers of immigrant children, as undocumented children being served in schools have often not been formally registered. As shown in Chapter Two, we have estimated that roughly 51,600 such children arrived from Mexico and the Northern Triangle countries alone between FY 2017 and FY 2019 and attend K–12 schools in California, whereas about 9,200 arrived during this time and attend K–12 schools in Louisiana. In addition, the two states have different levels and experience with ELLs. Roughly 19 percent of California's students are ELLs, while a little less than 4 percent of Louisiana's are ELLs (NCES, 2020).

The large variations in the numbers of newcomers and ELLs served within these two states have led to differences in policies and supports for those students, although political context and other factors come into play. California has many more policies than Louisiana to support the population of students studied in this report. First, California is a sanctuary state, by state law, with numerous sanctuary cities and counties that limit the extent to which local police take part in enforcing federal immigration laws, whereas Louisiana has one sanc-

Who We Interviewed in Case Study Schools

We interviewed nearly 40 district and school staff across our two case studies schools. The interviewees in Oakland Unified ($n = 21$) consisted of

- six central office staff
- principals and staff in three schools: one elementary school, one middle school, and one high school
- school staff, consisting of English-language development teachers, counselors, and social workers.

The interviewees in Jefferson Parish ($n = 17$) consisted of

- two central office staff
- principals and staff in three schools: one elementary school, one middle school, and one high school
- school staff, consisting of ESL coaches, educators, and counselors
- a community nongovernmental organization staff member serving the nonacademic needs of newcomer students through referrals from the schools.

tuary city: New Orleans (Vaughan and Griffith, 2021). In addition, California has numerous policies that support education and health outcomes among this population of children. For example, California offers in-state higher education tuition and financial aid, as well as health coverage, to all children, regardless of their immigration status, which is not the case in Louisiana (Williams, Figueroa, and Tharpe, 2019).

Overview of Two Case Study School Districts: Jefferson Parish in Louisiana and Oakland Unified in California

In this section, we provide an overview of demographics and the services and staffing for undocumented and asylum-seeking children in our two case study school systems: Louisiana's Jefferson Parish Schools and California's Oakland Unified School District.

Demographics

Table 4.1 provides an overview of the demographics for these two school districts. Both districts include between 80 and 90 schools in total, and roughly one-quarter of the families in both districts have incomes below the poverty level, based on American Community Survey data from 2018 (NCES, undated-a). However, Jefferson Parish is somewhat larger, as the nation's 98th largest school district, with roughly 49,862 students as of the 2019–2020 school year (Jefferson Parish Schools, undated), compared with Oakland Unified's 36,154 students in that same school year (NCES, undated-b). Oakland Unified is a city school district in the

TABLE 4.1

Student and Teacher Demographics in Jefferson Parish and Oakland Unified

School District	Oakland Unified	Jefferson Parish
Number of schools	87	84
Number of students	36,154	49,862
Number of teachers	1,911	2,363
Number of ELL students	11,990 (33%)	7,704 (15%)
Percentage of 5- to 17-year-olds in district who speak a language other than English at home	48%	20%
Among 5- to 17-year-olds who speak a language other than English at home, percentage speaking English less than "very well" according to family self-report	25%	26%
Percentage of non-English-speaking 5- to 17-year-olds in households with incomes below the poverty level	29%	29%

SOURCES: The numbers of schools, students, and teachers are based on data from NCES (undated-b) Common Core of Data for the 2019–2020 school year. Percentages of ELLs are also drawn from NCES Common Core of Data for the 2018–2019 school year. Percentages of students by English-language proficiency and by income below poverty level are from the American Community Survey District Dashboard, available through NCES (NCES, undated-a); the ACS measured English language proficiency levels through survey self-report.

heart of Oakland, California, whereas Jefferson Parish is a large suburban school district on the outskirts of New Orleans.

Although Oakland Unified serves fewer students than Jefferson Parish, a much larger proportion and number of Oakland Unified's students are ELLs. As of 2019, one-third of the total population of students in Oakland Unified (n = 11,990) were labeled ELLs, according to NCES (NCES, undated-b), which is about two times the proportion of ELLs (16 percent, or n = 7,704) in Jefferson Parish in that same year. By way of comparison, as of fall 2017, 5 million students were ELLs in the United States, the vast majority of whom were Hispanic or Latino, representing 10 percent of the nation's student population (NCES, 2020). And, as noted above, roughly 19 percent of the California student population, and a little less than 4 percent of the Louisiana student population, were labeled as ELLs during that same time period. Thus, both of our case study schools serve a much larger proportion of ELLs than a typical school district in their state or a typical school district in the United States. Both Alameda County (where Oakland Unified is located) and Jefferson Parish are in the top 50 counties in the United States in terms of the number of newcomers from Mexico and the Northern Triangle served by county schools, as shown in Table A.4.

According to Oakland Unified administrators, roughly one-quarter of the ELLs they serve are considered newcomer students who have been enrolled within the past three years. Between 80 and 90 percent of their ELLs qualify for FRL in a typical school year.[1] The home language of the large majority of Oakland Unified ELLs is Spanish, although staff note a growing population of students who speak Mam, an indigenous language of Guatemala. The top birth country of Oakland Unified students with a home language that is not English— beyond the United States—is Guatemala, followed by Mexico and El Salvador (Oakland Unified School District, 2018).

In Jefferson Parish, 86 percent of the ELLs are Spanish speakers; unlike Oakland Unified, Jefferson Parish does not collect data on immigration or country of origin from its students, although district and school staff noted to us that the largest proportion are from Honduras. The numbers of these students in middle and high school in Jefferson Parish have been growing faster than the numbers in elementary school. Teachers also noted their impression that more unaccompanied teens are arriving, while in the past most arrived with families.

Although Oakland Unified serves a larger proportion of ELLs than Jefferson Parish, Jefferson Parish has seen large growth in their ELL population. According to NCES (undated-b) Common Core of Data, Jefferson Parish served roughly 3,786 ELL students in the 2011–2012 school year (compared with 7,704 in 2019–2020), whereas Oakland Unified served 14,274 in 2011–2012 (compared with 11,990 in 2019–2020), which suggests that Jefferson Parish's ELL population has nearly doubled in a little less than a decade, whereas Oakland Unified ELL

---

[1] Proportions of newcomers who qualify for FRL in Oakland Unified should be interpreted with caution. According to Oakland Unified administrators who provided these data, newcomers who enroll midyear might not always be accurately identified as qualifying for FRL. Thus, these estimates may underrepresent actual FRL proportions.

Demographics in Case Study School Districts

ELLs in Oakland Unified School District:

- ELLs make up one-third of the district's student population (nearly 12,000 students)
- About 25% of ELLs have been enrolled in U.S. schools for three years or less
- ELLs mostly speak Spanish, although a growing proportion speak Mam, an indigenous language of Guatemala
- Between 80% and 90% of ELLs qualify for FRL in a typical year
- ELLs come from a large range of countries but the largest proportion's come from Guatemala, Mexico, and El Salvador

ELLs in Jefferson Parish:

- ELLs make up one-sixth of the district's student population (nearly 8,000 students)
- 39% of ELLs qualify for FRL
- 86% speak Spanish
- ELLs come from a range of countries, but the largest proportion comes from Honduras

population—along with overall enrollment—has decreased somewhat. According to Oakland Unified administrators with whom we spoke, that decrease is in large part due to rapid growth in Oakland's charter school sector.

Staffing and Services

Both Oakland Unified and Jefferson Parish have growing and developing services for their immigrant and ELL populations and dedicated staffing to provide those services. Here, we provide a brief description of these, with more in-depth discussions to follow, in our comparison of challenges and useful approaches.

Oakland Unified may have more-comprehensive support services for ELLs than almost any other school district in the nation. Indeed, several of the policy officials and heads of organizations in our interviews around the country identified Oakland Unified as a model for supporting undocumented and asylum-seeking children, as well as ELLs. The district's services for ELLs include the following:

- There are 114 teachers who primarily teach newcomers (i.e., have more than 50 percent newcomer students in their classrooms). Nearly all elementary teachers and many secondary teachers in Oakland Unified are also designated as providing at least some English-language development instruction and serve at least some newcomer or ELL students.
- The Office of English Language Learner and Multilingual Achievement is designed to support students' academic and nonacademic needs.

- The Office of Equity houses translation services and works to ensure inclusive fair conditions for all students.
- There are 17 schools designed to support newcomer students. The features of these schools include a focus on English-language development through certified ELL teachers, ESL coaches, extended learning opportunities designed for newcomers, and the availability of targeted services to meet the needs of newcomer students, including mental health and wellness services, family engagement, mentorship, legal assistance, and other services (Oakland Unified School District, undated).
- There are eight dual-language schools, the majority of which serve mostly ELL populations. Students who graduate with literacy in more than one language from any Oakland Unified school receive the "State Seal of Biliteracy" upon graduation.
- Newcomer immigrant students receive three years of concentrated ELL support, followed by additional help depending on their language proficiency.
- A growing number of teachers at elementary schools with 30 percent or more ELLs are certified in Guided Language Acquisition Design, and more than 100 teachers have bilingual authorization.
- Social workers in every secondary newcomer program support holistic needs of students.
- The community school model emphasizes partnerships with many outside services, including support for students' physical and mental health, legal services, and social services, as well as a range of other needs.

Jefferson Parish has a number of support services for ELLs and newcomer students, many of which have been more fully developed in recent years in response to growing numbers of such students. The district's services for ELLs include the following:

- There were 225 ELL teachers and 22 ELL staff in 2019–2020.
- One year of education through what Jefferson Parish calls its Newcomer Program, with 45 newcomer classrooms, provides survival English, American school norms, and soft skills to students who are new to the United States before students enter mainstream classrooms.
- ELL students in mainstream classrooms are supported by *paraprofessional* assistant teachers, who help with additional explanations and translations.
- Training and feedback from ESL coaches explain to teachers how to differentiate their instruction for the ELLs. All ESL coaches are trained in the Sheltered Instruction Observation Protocol, through the Center for Applied Linguistics. Additionally, ESL coaches participate in ongoing professional development and support in monthly sessions.
- ESL programs are provided through the Office of Multilingual Learning to support students in meeting state achievement standards and provide referrals for nonacademic services outside the classroom.

- There are ten dual-language magnet programs that teach half of the curriculum in English and half in Spanish, with native English and Spanish speakers.
- There are social workers and counselors in every school, with seven counselors bilingual in Spanish in the district.

Perspectives from Case Study District and School Staff on Challenges and Useful Approaches for Supporting This Population of Students

We next summarize potentially useful approaches and challenges for supporting undocumented and asylum-seeking children gleaned from interviews with central office and school staff in our two case study districts. Readers should keep in mind that these findings are necessarily limited by the virtue of who was included in our interview sample, and that sample was somewhat different in the two case study districts. In Oakland, we spoke with the district administrators who mainly provide support services for ELLs, as well as schools that have been intentionally designed to provide supports and services for Oakland's ELL population. By contrast, in Jefferson Parish, we spoke with district administrators who support the entire district (not just ELL populations), principals, teachers, counselors, and coaches in schools that serve all students, not specifically immigrant students more so than other students. Nevertheless, our findings offer helpful perspectives from a large number of administrators and educators who have been thinking long term about the best supports for newcomers.

Our findings are broken into sections related to (1) enrollment in school, (2) ELL and academics, (3) nonacademic supports, (4) teacher supports, and (5) state and district policy. Throughout, as appropriate, we integrate discussion of ways in which the COVID-19 pandemic has affected teaching and learning for undocumented and asylum-seeking children, as our interviews took place during the 2020–2021 school year. As we have noted, the pandemic has exacerbated many of the challenges such students face and has changed the nature of the work that district and school staff are doing to support these students. However, we focus mostly on broader issues that are related to supports for these students both before and beyond the pandemic. Table 4.2 summarizes the challenges and useful approaches related to these issues for the education of undocumented and asylum-seeking children.

Enrollment in School

Key Challenges

Interviewees in both districts acknowledged the importance of ensuring that all immigrant students—including those who are undocumented—can enroll in their district and receive ELL supports, as is legally required (see Chapter Three). At the same time, staff in both districts mentioned numerous challenges to enrolling students in school.

TABLE 4.2

Summary of Challenges and Useful Approaches Taken by Case Study Districts for the Education of Undocumented and Asylum-Seeking Children

Category	Challenges	Useful Approaches
Enrollment	• Language barriers for both parents and children, including barriers related to appropriate language testing and placement • Documentation requirements	• Guaranteed in-person enrollment with language supports for students and families • Simplified intake processes • Students referred to nonacademic services at the time of enrollment
English-language learning and academics	• Language barriers for children and teachers, including lack of bilingual staff for all languages spoken by children and large variation in English-language skills of incoming students • Difficulty in determining how and when to integrate newcomer ELLs into regular classrooms with students who speak English proficiently • Lack of good instructional materials and approaches for students who come to school far below their age-appropriate grade level, called students with interrupted formal education • Not enough support for undocumented students to pursue careers after high school	• Specific programs and supports for newcomer students • Treating language skills as an asset, including dual-language programs • Supportive high school models
Nonacademic supports	• The trauma and culture shock that many undocumented and asylum-seeking students are experiencing or have experienced • The poverty and lack of access to basic necessities among many students and their families • Weak family support at home for many students • Students' legal needs • Low attendance, truancy, and dropouts	• Approaches to build community and trust among students and families, as well as celebrate their diverse backgrounds and culture • Specialized staff to meet students' social and emotional needs • Referrals and partnerships with other community programs • Trauma-informed instruction that takes into account the challenges students have faced and their resilience to move beyond these challenges
Teacher training	• Need for teachers with expertise in language learning in Jefferson Parish • Need for specialized credentials to support approaches for dual languages and students with interrupted formal education	• Specialized staff who push in to support teachers • Intensive professional learning opportunities

Language Barriers

Staff in both districts noted language barriers with both parents and students as an obstacle to enrollment. Jefferson Parish had a shortage of administrative staff who could speak Spanish to communicate with parents and students. Although Oakland Unified had plenty of Spanish-speaking staff, it did not have enough interpreters for some of the other languages that enrolling students speak, including a growing population of students who speak Mam, an indigenous language of Guatemala. One principal commented that families of Mam-speaking students might not be literate in any language, so "it's not as simple as translating [written forms and information] into another language." These challenges have led to difficulties both in gathering necessary enrollment information from families and in language testing and placement into English-development classes. For example, although placement tests could be administered in Spanish, they might not be available for every language that incoming undocumented and asylum-seeking children speak (for example, some such students from the Northern Triangle speak indigenous languages), which limits accurate placement in classes that can provide the English-language support that students need.

Documentation Requirements

Both districts found that documentation requirements and online enrollment could hinder access to school for parents who speak little English, may be transient or struggle to produce required residency documentation, and have low computer literacy and access. Jefferson Parish found that gathering the paperwork necessary to prove residency (such as a light bill or lease) and immunization status was challenging for many. Indeed, studies of school districts in other states have also found that language barriers, paperwork processes, documentation requirements, and low computer literacy can hinder access to school for such students (Booi et al., 2016). Furthermore, parents in both Oakland Unified and Jefferson Parish often had concerns about sharing too much information about themselves, out of fear of immigration enforcement, although this issue came up more in Jefferson Parish. Online access was a particular challenge during the pandemic, when schools aimed to reduce in-person contact for such processes.

We described in Chapter Three how many districts around the country face the challenge of lack of knowledge about the law and good practice for requesting information for enrolling this population of students, but this issue did not arise in interviews in our case study schools, likely because both have extensive experience and large such populations and therefore are well versed in these issues.

Useful Approaches

The two school districts undertook a range of approaches to address these challenges.

Ensuring In-Person Enrollment with Language Supports for Immigrant Students and Families

Both districts developed approaches to work around the language and computer literacy challenges. Both have bilingual staff who can help families with the enrollment process, as well as other Spanish-language resources, although Oakland Unified has more such resources. In both districts, student enrollment shifted completely online at the start of the pandemic. However, because of concerns about computer literacy and access for some student populations, both districts kept some in-person enrollment during the 2020–2021 year. In the words of one administrator in Oakland Unified, "The shift has been having our staff understand that, while . . . emails might suffice for some families, for many of our immigrant families, we need to offer in-person office hours even if it means long lines. That's something we have to do."

Jefferson Parish combined student enrollment and language screening (with an English-language proficiency test) in one in-person location and offered parent liaisons to help with in-person registration, although administrators note that a shortage of bilingual staff remains an obstacle to supporting students in general. Oakland Unified included a staff of numerous Spanish speakers to accommodate and interpret for Spanish-speaking families and has also produced videos in multiple languages that families can access, particularly those that might not be literate in English or any language, although those videos might not be accessible to all families. Yet, multiple people with whom we spoke in Oakland noted that they particularly have challenges in identifying Mam speakers who can serve as translators for the growing Mam-speaking Guatemalan population coming into the district.

Simplified Intake Processes

Both districts simplified processes for enrollment, aiming to collect enough information to place the children while not requesting information that families might consider threatening to their immigration status. Therefore, the enrollment process does not require documentation of citizenship or Social Security numbers, although some documents that prove local residency (such as a lease or utility bill) and immunization status are required, and others, such as birth certificates and school transcripts (when available), are requested. In both districts, immigration status is not explicitly discussed during intake, although—as discussed below—Oakland Unified asks families a much larger range of questions related to health insurance and legal and other services that are available to undocumented and asylum-seeking students. Perhaps partially because such a large range of services is not available in Jefferson Parish, and because administrators indicated that they do not wish to deter families from enrolling their children, Jefferson Parish interviewees particularly stressed that they avoided questioning students about their immigration status. In the words of one Jefferson administrator: "We are not going to dig too deep into your personal business. We are here for teaching and learning."

Referring Students to Some Nonacademic Services at the Time of Enrollment

Oakland Unified uses the enrollment process to link students and families to a comprehensive range of other supports, while Jefferson Parish keeps enrollment processes limited to academic and immunization requirements. A staff member in the Oakland Unified English Language Learner and Multilingual Achievement office described their approach as a "community school model," since they manage so many partnerships with outside services. In

Oakland Unified, central office staff ask enrolling students and their families questions, often with the aid of translators, about their need for housing, medical insurance, social services, transportation, and legal services to support the issues they may be facing. Jefferson Parish does have an immunization bus that provides an easier way for students to obtain the immunizations they need to enroll in school. But, on balance, Jefferson Parish asks fewer questions to students and families about the broad range of needs they may have. Because California is a sanctuary state, answering these questions is likely lower risk for parents, while—according to the Jefferson Parish district staff with whom we spoke—many parents of these students in Louisiana perceive discussing immigration status in Louisiana, which is not a sanctuary state, as having some risk. These different approaches also reflect the greater availability of services for undocumented students in California compared with Louisiana, whereas there is a more limited system of networks between school staff and community services to support these students. For example, because medical insurance is available to undocumented students and families, Oakland Unified helps with the completion of insurance paperwork.

English-Language Learning and Academics

Key Challenges

Critical challenges for English-language learning and academics in both districts were language barriers (mainly in Louisiana), questions about when students are ready to be integrated into regular classrooms, lack of resources to support enrolling students with gaps in their formal education, and limited postsecondary options for students.

Language Barriers

One of the main challenges raised repeatedly in Jefferson Parish was the "language barrier," as the district has relatively few bilingual staff and struggles to find bilingual and ESL-certified teachers. Teachers in Jefferson reported that it could take several years for students to adapt to English and that this was particularly challenging for older students. Noting a common concern, one teacher said that "it is hard to stay motivated" because of communication difficulties.

In Oakland, concerns about language barriers mainly came up in reference to the growing Mam-speaking population. One staff member noted that some families who speak Mam might not be literate in any language, so "it's not as simple as translating into another language." Because many incoming Mam students have not attended formal education previously, they may need intensive language support that is not available to them because of the lack of Mam speakers in the district.

How and When to Integrate Newcomer English-Language Learners into Regular Classrooms with Students Who Speak English Proficiently

In both districts, staff described the challenge of determining when to integrate newcomer ELLs into regular classrooms with students who speak English proficiently. For many years, Jefferson Parish had a program that pulled ELLs out of regular classrooms for separate instruction, since those who were put in regular classrooms were overwhelmed. But, according to one Jefferson Parish educator, newcomer children who had participated in this pull-out model would often feel "alienated" from the other children, and some "totally shut down." Furthermore, the pull-out program did not present as much rich grade-level content as mainstream classrooms, and, as the newcomer population grew, the district could not find enough qualified Spanish-speaking teachers for this approach, according to those with whom we spoke. Similarly, Oakland Unified staff noted that students may struggle after being integrated into classes with non-ELL peers, even after several years of ELL instruction, posing challenges for both the students and their teachers.

Lack of Quality Instructional Materials and Approaches for Students Who Come to School Far Below Their Age-Appropriate Grade Level

Interviewees in both districts described a lack of adequate solutions for the students with interrupted formal education, some of whom enroll in school with little prior formal education, sometimes testing into an academic level many years below their age-appropriate grade level. One Jefferson Parish teacher explained, "They haven't acquired the basics that the rest of the children have. And so it is not just a language barrier to skills, because they don't have the skills. . . . They can't count to 20, some of them." In both districts, grade-level placement is typically based on age in combination with assessed grade level. Jefferson Parish staff repeatedly noted the lack of available assessments in Spanish to determine the grade level of incoming students and particularly students with interrupted formal education. Beyond placement tests, educators in both districts also commented on not having adequate resources, practices, or assessments for these students, although both mentioned turning to resources provided by the state of New York for students with interrupted formal education. As one Oakland Unified teacher said, "It's nearly impossible for a classroom teacher of 29 kids to support a student who needs support to catch up five to six years." Jefferson educators also noted that teachers struggle with these gaps; one described needing to circle back to foundational skills that are required to understand lessons: "For example, we are covering the slope of a line, and they don't remember how to add fractions, and you have to go back to fractions."

Not Enough Support for Undocumented Students to Pursue Careers After High School

School staff in both districts also reported some challenges in helping students consider post-secondary education options. First, they noted that some students and families expected that students would enter the workforce both during high school and immediately after; sometimes, heavy work schedules during high school could place learning and graduation at risk. Second, vocational programs do not exist that would prepare these students for the jobs that are available to them, given lack of English fluency, being behind grade level, or lacking documentation required for some jobs. Third, students with interrupted formal education in particular entered school so far below grade level that it was difficult for school staff to see how these students might catch up and graduate. Lastly, administrators in both districts communicated some frustration that students did not always qualify for higher-education opportunities that are available for other students, although the concerns in districts differed, given the differences in state laws for Louisiana and California in this regard. In Jefferson Parish, administrators said that students need a Social Security number to enroll in the career pathway certifications required for some high school course pathways or to get a GED. However, undocumented students often do not have that ID and thus do not have access to those opportunities. In California, students who are undocumented qualify for in-state tuition if they have been in California three years or more, but they do not qualify for some of the aid provided to other immigrant students, and so they often have very limited college options.

Useful Approaches

The two districts took several approaches to address these challenges, although they acknowledge that these approaches do not fully meet needs and that significant gaps still remain.

Specific Programs and Supports for Newcomer Students

Both districts offer a separate program for newcomer students, who are entering a U.S. school for the first time and do not speak English. Students in Jefferson Parish receive one year of newcomer instruction. In Oakland Unified, students have a longer entrance ramp into regular classroom instruction, including their three years of intensive newcomer support and some content instruction alongside other ELLs.

To address the deficiencies of previous pull-out approaches of integrating ELL newcomer students, Jefferson Parish piloted and then shifted in the 2019–2020 school year to a more inclusive model that provides newcomer students with one year of separate instruction and then integrates them into the regular student population. The district developed this approach by relying on practices they learned about from the Council of Great City Schools, a coalition that brings together the largest American urban school districts to improve education. Students in the one-year newcomer program learn basic skills to become familiar with school expectations and schedules, survival English, and soft skills that build their self-esteem. The majority of educators at these newcomer schools are bilingual and receive professional development specifically to support instruction in English-language development. Staff in Jefferson Parish spoke of the newcomer program as an improvement over the pull-out model, but the transition out of the newcomer model and into the regular classroom was still "challenging and exhausting" for students, particularly for those students coming to school with little formal education. In the words of one educator, newcomer students "are not performing at the same level as their peers, but they're filling those gaps much faster than if we just put them in isolation."

In Jefferson Parish, interviewees spoke of two main strategies to support students' English learning in the classroom. First, content teachers focus on differentiating their instruction, using multiple ways to explain concepts to reach students at different levels in their classrooms, using visual aids, and teaching students to use translation websites. One educator noted that one silver lining of the pandemic was a district policy to provide all students with devices that enabled some ELLs to better access translation or bilingual resources. Second, the district has one Spanish-speaking paraprofessional per grade level in each school. In the classroom, the paraprofessionals provide additional support to ELL students, translating, repeating instructions, or reexplaining concepts in Spanish. Several Jefferson Parish interviewees commented that, if they had one wish, it would be for more paraprofessionals to provide one-to-one support for ELL students within the regular classrooms.

Incoming students who enroll at Oakland Unified are often placed in one of 18 schools intended to support newcomer students: three elementary schools, eight middle schools, six high schools, and one continuation school—that are specifically designed to support newcomer students. The features of these schools include a focus on English-language development, extended learning opportunities designed for newcomers, and targeted services to meet the needs of newcomer students, including mental health and wellness services, family engagement, mentorship, legal assistance, and other services (Oakland Unified School District, undated). One Oakland Unified staff member referred to the district's approach as a "community schools" model.

Some newcomer students are placed outside these newcomer schools because of family preference or other reasons. Oakland Unified schools beyond those 17 offer a range of universal supports for ELLs, including at least two required periods of English-language development, extended learning opportunities, and counseling, among other supports. According to our interviews, a growing number of Oakland Unified elementary schools are offering at least some specialized newcomer supports; 14 school sites were planning to offer such supports in 2021–2022.

Treating Language Skills and Diverse Experiences as an Asset, Including Dual-Language Programs

Both districts aimed to view the Spanish-language skills of the ELLs as an opportunity and resource in different ways. As noted by one Jefferson Parish educator, "The language is the best part because I think we can all benefit. . . . Our students in general can benefit from interacting with students from diverse countries and different cultures. . . . They expose everybody else to other things, which makes it more global."

Both districts offer dual-language programs. Jefferson Parish provides a dual-language magnet program for children in grades kindergarten through second; this is a program that provides literacy and content instruction to all students (both native English speakers and native Spanish speakers) through two languages. The district plans to expand this by a grade per year as students in the program advance. This program originally started out as a French program based on Louisiana's French heritage but now includes Spanish. One interviewee at Jefferson Parish commented that, although English-speaking families have high demand for the dual-language program, they sometimes have to try hard to recruit Spanish-speaking families because those families are worried that such a program might disadvantage their child if the child is not fully immersed in an English-language classroom.

Oakland Unified interviewees also laid out to us the benefits of providing dual-language programs that include instruction in both English and Spanish, and district documentation notes that dual-language approaches have a better research base for improving ELL than other approaches (Oakland Unified School District, undated). The school system has eight dual-language schools, the majority of which serve mostly ELL populations. Students who graduate with literacy in more than one language from any Oakland Unified school receive the "State Seal of Biliteracy" upon graduation. One Oakland Unified administrator noted that the seal helps teachers avoid the trap of thinking that students cannot handle high-level content and also helps them to view students' native language skills as valuable.

The idea of treating students' background and experiences as critical assets to support them and their education was also brought up in both districts when discussing ways in which teachers support students both academically and socially and emotionally (as we discuss more in later sections of this chapter). For example, a principal in Oakland Unified stressed the need to "elevate and make more visible Mam language and culture" so that students were more comfortable speaking Mam in school, which is important for both their academic and their linguistic development. Another interviewee from Jefferson Parish noted that learning more about students' countries and cultures shows students that educators are "invested" in them. By supporting students culturally, educators believe that their students have a better chance of excelling academically.

Supportive High School Models

Both districts have done some thinking about the types of college and career readiness that newcomer ELLs might need most. Oakland Unified, in particular, has several high schools intended to support immigrant students, including an international school and a continuation school that is specifically intended to support older students who might not have parental support at home. However, staff also acknowledged that those programs might not support all of students' college and career needs. For example, several high schools in Oakland Unified provide the opportunity for only one career focus, which may limit students' options. One principal at a high school wondered why high schools cannot work together to offer multiple career programs to support the needs and interests of their diverse student populations. In Jefferson Parish, educators struggled with how best to prepare these students for the workplace after high school. Although the district offers career and technical education pathways that are available to these students, educators told us that new graduation pathways were needed, in particular for students with interrupted formal education, in ways that incorporated English-language, math, and job skills in the classroom and that supported such students in graduating. Staff were concerned that students sometimes did not have access to the vocational programs that could prepare them for a career after high school if they were not planning to go to college.

Oakland Unified's continuation high school is intended specifically to support unaccompanied students. The school includes students who get special supports and adults who care for them after the students turn 18, and they can continue at the school until they are 21 or even 22 years old. In describing this program, one school administrator noted, "We ask, what do you need to graduate? How will we get you those needs? We have a full-time social worker, a case manager, a drug counselor. . . . [We also provide] PE [physical education] credits for the jobs students do, like house cleaning."

Supporting Nonacademic Needs

Key Challenges

The nonacademic challenges that undocumented and asylum-seeking children face came up numerous times in both districts, including issues related to trauma and culture shock, lack of access to basic necessities, weak family support at home, students' legal issues, and resulting absenteeism among students. All immigrant students do not face these challenges; undocumented children—in particular—may be more likely to face them because of their relative lack of access to resources, their home-life circumstances, and the circumstances in their home countries that they have sought to escape.

The Trauma and Culture Shock That Many Undocumented and Asylum-Seeking Students Are Experiencing or Have Experienced

Staff in both districts commented on the trauma students might have experienced in their home countries or as a result of their journeys to the United States. As one Oakland Unified principal commented, "The kids are dealing with so many intense emotions. So much death here, at home. . . . It's horrifying." Staff in Jefferson Parish commented that "the students come with a lot of trauma" related to experiences in their home countries, assaults during their journeys to the United States, or unsettled home lives. As newcomers, students often "feel like an outsider" and have a "sense of not belonging" in school or in the United States. Administrators and counselors noted themselves struggling emotionally because of the horrific issues that they heard about repeatedly from the students.

Several educators in both districts noted that these students might not understand norms and expectations regarding schooling, especially if they lacked formal education in their home countries. For example, educators in Jefferson Parish and Oakland Unified noted that students might not be comfortable speaking up in class or making eye contact because of the trauma they have experienced, not feeling confident in speaking English or knowing the answers in their new environment, and norms for showing respect to adults in their countries. Oakland Unified staff expressed the concern that students from rural areas in Central America without access to comprehensive systems of formal education may have significant gaps in basic numeracy and literacy, which complicate attempts to provide grade-level, content-area instruction.

Poverty and Lack of Access to Basic Necessities Among Many Students and Their Families

Food insecurity and medical needs were also mentioned by staff in both districts as common issues for some undocumented and asylum-seeking children and their families, with our interviewees noting that these issues have been exacerbated by the COVID-19 pandemic. In Oakland Unified, in particular, the expense of housing was mentioned as an issue, and a principal in Jefferson Parish explained that job losses during the pandemic meant that some students lacked electricity needed to charge devices provided by the school district for remote learning. As one teacher noted, "Many [students] are living in one room that they don't have legal rights to or are renting out part of an apartment." In the pandemic, in particular, students may be in living environments that do not support their learning, such as multifamily apartments. In both Oakland Unified and Jefferson Parish, teachers talked about students' hesitancy to be on video during remote learning, which they guessed was in part because of students' living conditions.

Families Struggling to Provide for Students' Educational Needs

Relatedly, many undocumented and asylum-seeking children face challenges because they lack sufficient adult support at home, challenges that other students do not face. Migration circumstances have created conditions in which families might not have the ability to readily support their children's educational needs. For example, parents of some of these children may be working very long hours and therefore cannot supervise or prioritize their children's education, as described by staff in both districts. As one teacher in Oakland Unified said to us, "Kids are sometimes coming here with—for example—just dad, who is working 12 to 14 hour days, and it's hard. They don't have the same kind of support at home. Sometimes it feels like they don't have both that academic support and also the emotional support." A Jefferson Parish staff member noted that some undocumented and asylum-seeking children have extensive responsibilities at home, such as cooking, cleaning, and being caregivers for others, and they "all have keys around their necks" because, for some children, no adult is present when they get home from school. In addition, some parents may struggle to help their children with their homework when they are home, especially if they have not had as much formal education themselves or have limited English proficiency.

These challenges can be particularly intense for students who have come to the United States unaccompanied, as unaccompanied children are placed with sponsor families, often relatives or others they do not know well and who sometimes are not taking good care of them, as related by staff in both districts. These children may be passed among different households or live with parents they had not seen in years prior to arrival. One Oakland Unified staff member noted that the lack of support is particularly acute for unaccompanied minors because they are "dealing with a lot of other things that a lot of people their age don't deal with, like immigration court."

Students' Legal Needs

Several administrators and educators in Oakland Unified commented that the Trump administration had made legal processes for undocumented immigrants much more difficult to navigate. One district administrator noted that immigration policies place a lot of stress on students because the policies are frequently changing, and there is a lack of clarity on what families should be doing. Jefferson Parish did not report as much involvement as Oakland Unified in students' legal circumstances, as the district lacks similar legal resources. However, interviewees mentioned some children coming to school upset or fearful over a parent's deportation. One counselor tried to explain children's feelings: "You don't know if you go back home and if your parents are going to be there. They went to work, and they could be caught by immigration officers for ICE."

Local immigrant enforcement may actually drive students and their families out of and away from schools. In Oakland Unified, central office staff mentioned the trainings that they offer to all staff to provide information about what it means for Oakland to be a sanctuary city, along with the protocols they should follow in the case of any ICE intervention. One study between 2000 and 2011 of 55 counties in the United States that had partnerships between ICE and local police for immigration enforcement found that the number of Hispanic students enrolled in schools dropped by 10 percent two years after the partnership was enacted. Enrollment drops were concentrated among elementary school students, many of whom were U.S. citizens, as families moved to avoid this (Dee and Murphy, 2019).

Low Attendance, Truancy, and Dropouts

Staff in both districts noted that these challenges often result in attendance issues. In Jefferson Parish, educators repeatedly described attendance issues as one of the biggest challenges with some of their immigrant population in general, along with many other student populations during the pandemic. District staff noted high rates of absenteeism and dropouts, particularly among high school students. As one Jefferson Parish counselor said, "We have a lot of missing kids." Administrators mentioned that tools available to them to manage attendance, such as reporting truancy to local officials, were often not effective or "could open a whole other can of worms" because of a family's undocumented status.

Reasons given for the high rates of absenteeism were the transience of families that moved for work, caretaking by children for other family members, inability of parents to enforce attendance, overwhelmed students in the new school environment, and, in the case of high school students, competing work schedules. As one high school principal in Jefferson Parish tried to explain in reference to some of the undocumented and asylum-seeking children the district serves:

> They're bringing in money and it's supporting their family now. It might not be a whole lot, but to them it's money and it's survival. It's almost like survival in Maslow's hierarchy of needs. You know, it's food, water, air, shelter. That's where we are basically with these kids. And where does education fit in their hierarchy?

Useful Approaches

Both districts have put numerous supports in place to address students' nonacademic needs, including efforts to improve trust between district staff, students, and families; partnerships with community services; and various social and emotional supports.

Approaches to Build Trust Among Students and Families and Celebrate Their Culture

Staff in both districts repeatedly noted the importance of acknowledging students' culture and making students feel comfortable about their culture at school. An Oakland Unified principal mentioned working to elevate the Mam culture and making it more visible, mostly because of noticing that some students were embarrassed to speak Mam or reveal to others that they were Mam speakers. Similarly, a Jefferson Parish educator said, "We create the opportunities for these children to talk to each other about their experiences, so they know they are not alone." Another administrator in Oakland talked particularly about grounding education for undocumented and asylum-seeking children in a positive perspective of those students:

> Everything begins with understanding that immigrant students and families have a lot to offer, and they come with unique gifts and talents. Start off with embracing immigrant students and families, instead of seeing them as a burden and as overwhelming. Instead, it's how do we see immigrant students and families as gifts to our school communities, to our cities, and really embracing the culture and traditions and languages that are coming into our schools—how is this diversity benefiting our school community?

Both districts similarly emphasized the importance of building relationships with students. As one principal in Jefferson Parish said, "If they know they can trust you, they will. They will bend over backwards to try to please you. And I always love going to their rooms to reground. . . . They're always so happy just to be here. . . . I'm positive I'd be lifted up a little bit. . . . [It brings out] the compassionate side of teachers because they understand the struggle." In both districts, staff also reach out to immigrant families regularly through notes and phone calls. Schools in Jefferson Parish also make efforts to include children in sports and clubs, including creating activity funds that can "troubleshoot financially" to give children the resources they need to join such activities. Additionally, a bilingual social worker or administrator in Jefferson makes calls to parents about attendance and other issues; during the pandemic, school communities organized to ensure that all students had access to food. They also offer computer skill workshops for parents in English and Spanish.

The Office of Equity in Oakland Unified specifically asks the principal of each school to assign a teacher leader and parent leader to parent action teams that develop a family partnership plan for the school, including what it means to build relationships with families and communicate transparently with them. The Office of Equity has also held family events to communicate to immigrant families about the policies and protocols the district has developed for communicating with ICE. In the words of one administrator from the Office of Equity,

> Direct communication . . . [has a] direct relationship to student attendance and subsequent academic outcomes. Through academic communication, there's trust instilled on both sides—build on family and educator sides. It begins to inform this mentality that we can't do this without each other. That's really the culture that we're trying to build.

Specialized Staff to Meet Students' Social and Emotional Needs

Both districts also have a set of specialized staff to support students' nonacademic needs, including social and emotional well-being. Oakland Unified's English Language Learner and Multilingual Achievement office has a program manager for newcomer wellness who manages a team of social workers for newcomer schools, and each secondary newcomer program is provided with a social worker. Jefferson Parish also provides social workers and counselors in every school who can also support students' needs. Throughout the district, there are seven bilingual counselors, a number that was not viewed by interviewees as sufficient, given the needs. One principal noted, "We don't really have a lot of emotional support. We don't have enough social workers or counselors to really help the students go through the process."

Referrals and Partnerships with Other Community Programs
Oakland Unified has more of a range of supports for newcomers and ELLs in-house than Jefferson Parish, although both districts have networks on which they rely for referrals. Oakland Unified has a program manager who oversees all newcomer and refugee student enrollment and referrals to services, including help signing up for medical insurance, social workers, and interpreters. In one example, Oakland Unified's enrollment system ensures that students are assigned legal and other supports that they need. One administrator at Oakland Unified noted:

> [We] have turned into paralegals to fill out asylum applications, appeal forms for students with removal orders, and are trying to learn as much as possible as we can about the immigration process. All of us have been in immigration court, to the ICE office to accompany students for check-ins. It's always on our mind, the changing immigration policies.

Oakland Unified staff keep track of unaccompanied minors when they enroll and continue to refer them to immigration attorneys "until someone takes their case." Administrators noted that, in the past, students had to drop out and get stressed about paying attorneys, as well as going to attorneys who were not reputable. Even with these many services, some at Oakland Unified commented that students' needs are still often unmet. In the words of one district administrator, "It's a glass half empty, glass half full kind of thing. We're focused on how far we have to go within Oakland Unified, but when we step out of the district, we realized we have a lot."

Both Oakland Unified and Jefferson Parish also maintain a network of outside resources to which they can refer students. For Jefferson Parish, that includes organizations with Spanish-speaking counselors and attorneys, including Catholic Charities and community groups that can help students receive health coverage through Medicaid, when they qualify. According to Louisiana law, refugee and asylum-seeking children are eligible, although some noncitizens are not (State of Louisiana, 2021). Oakland Unified administrators note that they often refer students to doctors and dentists, as well as immigration attorneys and other social service support.

Trauma-Informed Instruction
Lastly, in Oakland Unified, staff spoke frequently about the need to provide *trauma-informed instruction* that supports students' social and emotional needs. Although that term did not come up in Jefferson Parish, educators there noted the importance of sensitivity toward these children and relationship building. Some descriptions among Oakland Unified staff about what trauma-informed instruction means:

- "making a safe space for the students"
- "having a very consistent routine and schedule, but also having some flexibility"
- "not responding [to misbehavior] in a way that is reactive and thinking about what the student is thinking about in that situation[,] . . . not responding [in] a way that confirms what they're thinking about themselves in that moment, like 'I'm bad' or 'I'm disrespect-ful.'"

One Oakland Unified school leader noted that the district's adoption of a "trauma-informed services perspective" has reduced classroom conflict and improved school culture and climate. Another principal noted that these approaches to supporting students are closely aligned with social and emotional learning approaches and commented, "There has been a shift from social and emotional learning as a nice thing we can do to 'it is a central part of schooling' . . . with this population [of students]. It cannot be a side thought. It has to be embedded in every teachers' policies, every event we have, a social emotional healing approach."

Teacher Training and Supports

Key Challenges

Staff in both districts talked about the need for more teacher training, although the conversations in those districts were different, given the variation in training and skills among the staff in the two districts.

Need for Teachers with Expertise in English-Language Learning

In Jefferson Parish, most teachers with newcomer students in their classrooms are not bilingual and do not typically have ELL certification, and several administrators commented on the challenge of recruiting and hiring teachers who have been trained to support English learning. Administrators also noted that they often encourage teachers to get certification to work with ELLs, but teachers find it very difficult to acquire the certification while they are working, and most teachers did not have this training as part of their teacher college preparation. As a result, Jefferson Parish administrators have observed that many teachers struggle with English-language acquisition techniques and strategies and get frustrated by all that is being asked of them in the classroom. One described the challenges felt by teachers: "They have a lot on their plate and are pulled to do many things."

Need for Specialized Credentials to Support Dual-Language and Approaches for Students with Interrupted Formal Education

Oakland Unified administrators did not speak about the lack of bilingual teachers or teachers with some ESL training. However, they did describe the challenge of ensuring that teachers have the more-specialized credentials they need to support dual-language approaches and to support students with interrupted formal education. In Oakland Unified, all teachers—not just those in newcomer schools—are required to have ELL certification. And, in California, teacher certification programs include some preparation to teach ELLs. Furthermore,

California teachers of courses provided in languages other than English are required to have authorization in Bilingual, Cross-Cultural, Language and Academic Development (BCLAD). However, one teacher noted a belief that the ELL and BCLAD certifications are not enough for teachers, who need more knowledge and experience, as well as more approaches to dual-language education and approaches for students with interrupted formal education. Another teacher mentioned borrowing a lot of materials from the New York State Department of Education's resources for students with interrupted formal education but does not have training to use those resources and wishes they had that training. Other principals and administrators at Oakland Unified noted that specialized training is a necessity for teachers who have to work with undocumented and asylum-seeking children, who often have diverse needs.

Useful Approaches

Useful approaches to supporting teachers of ELLs mentioned by case study districts included providing more-specialized staff and coaching, as well as more-intensive professional learning opportunities.

Providing Specialized Staff Who Push in to Support Teachers

Each district has specialized staff who push in to support ELLs within teachers' classrooms as they are teaching all students (as opposed to pulling ELLs out of the classroom for specialized instruction apart from their peers). In Jefferson Parish, for example, teachers and administrators noted that ESL coaches provide training, professional development, and feedback for regular classroom teachers with ELLs. The coaching cycle consists of training, observation, and postobservation feedback. One coach described the role with teachers: "We meet as a little cluster twice a month. . . . I may give them one or two strategies to try out. And then they go back and work with the kids with those strategies and then come back and we debrief and talk about what worked and what didn't work." Similarly, Oakland Unified provides central office language specialists who support all schools in developing and delivering professional learning to support ELL instruction.

Providing Intensive Professional Learning Opportunities

In addition, each district has established intensive professional learning opportunities, although those opportunities are sometimes expensive and difficult to offer consistently. One of the activities that an interviewee from Oakland Unified's English Language Learner and Multilingual Achievement office described as the "bread and butter" of the office is professional development. That staff member emphasized the importance of trained staff who can support newcomer students: "Their needs are different. . . . [The] reality is that it requires specialized staff and instruction." But the office does not always have funding to provide the intensive professional development opportunities teachers may need, and it sometimes leverages external funding for these opportunities. For example, several teachers and administrators in Oakland Unified noted the usefulness of a recent lesson study series supported by one local foundation that offered teachers paid opportunities after school on Saturdays; the teachers would pick an instructional topic, make a video of their classroom instruction, and then bring it back to the group to discuss. In the words of one teacher, this opportunity provided "a really collaborative learning space to think about our newcomers. . . . [It was a] really nice space to think more strategically . . . about how to support newcomers with a very narrow focus about where we want to see them improve." The administrators who provided this opportunity acknowledged that it is a really important one but also an expensive one that requires funding. They received funding in past years to offer this opportunity but have not yet obtained funding for such an opportunity this year.

Funding and Accountability as Federal Policy Challenges

Although we asked district educators and staff mainly about the challenges and useful approaches related to the educational needs of this population of students, interviewees also spoke about broader state and federal policies that create challenges to their everyday work in schools. These challenges include the ways in which schools are resourced to support these students.

Funding Levels and Schedules

Interviewees in both districts spoke about various obstacles that keep them from acquiring the funding they need to support newcomer students—especially those newcomers with intensive needs. In Oakland Unified, one key funding challenge mentioned to us was the requirement that enrollment counts are provided at the beginning of the year to determine funding for all students for the remainder of the year. As noted by several administrators, Oakland Unified often experiences surges in enrollment that are unpredictable and would likely require, as one administrator explained, "some sort of mechanism [which does not exist right now] by which districts would be adequately resourced to receive large numbers of students midyear." Another administrator wished that there would be some recognition from the state that there are "particular communities and districts that are the recipients of large waves of immigration due the particular immigration patterns. . . . There needs to be more nimbleness and flexibility."

Fluctuating enrollment patterns also cause challenges for the schools. In November 2020, Oakland Unified administrators commented that the flow of undocumented and asylum-seeking children had nearly come to a standstill since the start of the pandemic. For example, one administrator noted that, until March 2020, Oakland Unified enrolled an average of a little more than 20 unaccompanied minors per month, and roughly that many family cases. However, when we spoke to these administrators in November 2020, they spoke of enrolling only about 30 unaccompanied minors and a handful of family cases since March. They expressed concern that this might indicate that pent-up migration demand from the pandemic could result in a later surge, since start-of-year enrollment determines school funding. Data provided to us by Jefferson Parish reflect the same trend, with the number of high school students in the newcomer program dropping from 485 in 2019–2020 to 335 in 2020–2021 and the number of middle school newcomers dropping from 383 to 207 in that same period. The circumstances in the two case study districts reflect similar national drops in people coming across the border, as discussed in Chapter One.

In addition, administrators in both districts noted the dilemma of unduplicated count requirements. Specifically, districts are able to get more funding for enrolled students who are ELLs, low-income students, or foster youth. But students cannot be doubly counted in any of those categories. So, in the words of one district administrator:

> A newcomer from Germany whose dad is a professor at Caltech generates the same funding as an unaccompanied youth from Guatemala who is illiterate and walked here. . . . The unduplicated count, we wish it was duplicated so we were more intensively resourced to service students who [may be experiencing multiple disadvantages—e.g., are both low income and ELLs].

Although administrators in both districts appreciated the funding that has been provided through Title I and Title III of ESSA to support immigrant students, those in both districts also noted that funding does not support the needs of all students because it focuses mostly on students' academic needs, despite the wide range of needs that these students have. In Jefferson Parish, they interviewees that, although they can use Title I and Title III funding for some of the district's ESL coaches, available federal resources do not cover most of their needs, and they pay for most of the expenses for their coaches, ESL teachers, and paraprofessionals through their general funds. In Oakland Unified, administrators talked about various funding streams that have supported their work beyond what is provided through Title I and Title III. This funding has been procured through grants that administrators have applied for, including a foundation grant of $100,000 each year to support professional development for teachers (although the district has not received that support this past year) and a $600,000 yearly grant through the California Department of Social Services to support unaccompanied minors and refugee students (California Department of Social Services, undated). This funding has been critical to allowing Oakland Unified to provide all the supports it is able to provide, yet it is not necessarily a sustained funding stream.

Policy Guidance

Both districts expressed concern about the lack of policy clarity on some issues with regard to these students. Oakland Unified staff spoke in many of our interviews about the importance of being a sanctuary district in a sanctuary state, which allows them to talk to undocumented and asylum-seeking children and families in a more open way about the supports they need and what is available. In Jefferson Parish, administrators noted a lack of guidance at the state level about certain policy issues, with one saying, "There's so much variety and there's no real clear guidance from the state as far as expectations." Interviewees from both districts expressed a desire for more policy guidance, curriculum resources, and other supports for their students with interrupted formal education. Those in Jefferson Parish in particular noted the need for alternative graduation pathways for students with interrupted formal education and more-technical courses.

Accountability Challenges

Jefferson Parish staff, in particular, communicated concern about accountability requirements in Louisiana. Jefferson Parish staff commented on accountability concerns for ELLs more so than their counterparts at Oakland Unified did. Specifically, newcomer ELLs are to be included in school achievement calculations after one year of newcomer preparation, which many in Jefferson Parish feel is unfair to both students and teachers. No one with whom we spoke in Oakland Unified articulated that concern, although newcomer students there are also not required to take the state English-language arts standardized test in the first 12 months of their enrollment (although they must take the state mathematics test).

Summary

The challenges that undocumented and asylum-seeking children face are considerable and wide ranging, from academic and language learning to challenges related to needs that affect academic work in school. Immigration status exacerbates all those challenges by limiting the resources available to newcomers and raising legal challenges.

Both districts provide these students with numerous resources and supports, including those related to access and enrollment, ELL, and academics; nonacademic supports, such as supporting students socially and emotionally; services to meet students' basic and legal needs; and teacher training. Both districts have developed thoughtful approaches to providing ELLs with at least some support specific to their newcomer needs, such as dual-language approaches, and some initial period in which they focus on newcomer education without being overwhelmed by being in classes with their English-speaking peers.

At the same time, these districts acknowledge that all these resources do not fully meet the needs of undocumented and asylum-seeking children, particularly students who might not have sufficient family support at home and those who have come into the district with gaps in their formal education. Funding and accountability policies may create obstacles to providing those supports. Because California is a sanctuary state that provides some services to all children—such as health insurance and access to higher education—regardless of their immigration status, Oakland Unified links school enrollment with other supports. Yet those policies may also place larger burdens on the school system to ensure that students are taking advantage of those services, even though state and federal funding for schools does not include financial assistance to support these efforts.

CHAPTER FIVE

Recommendations, Conclusions, and Implications

In this report, we have found that growing numbers of undocumented and asylum-seeking children are arriving in the United States, estimating that 321,000 enrolled in U.S. schools from FYs 2017 through 2019. Federal law establishes the rights of these children to public education. The two case study school districts that we considered were making efforts to provide quality education for this population and address challenges through innovating and learning. At the same time, gaps remain in the supports needed in the education of these newcomers. Here, we offer recommendations to federal and state policymakers, as well a school districts.

Developing Policies and Processes to Address the Initial Needs of Children and Youth When They Cross the Border

Develop and Improve Definitions, Data, and Information Sources

Data about the numbers, locations, and ages of undocumented and asylum-seeking children are not available to the extent needed to support policymaking, as evidenced by the fact that we had to develop models for this project. Some information is available about children encountered at the border and at various steps of processing by DHS, DOJ, and HHS; however, then there is a gap in the data about how these children fare in schools. Furthermore, information is not available at a national level or in a comparable way across states about what approaches states are taking in the education of this population. Relatedly, there is no set of standard or accepted terms or definitions related to this population to make cross-state comparisons possible, as evidenced by the varying terms and definitions we found in our case studies. We recommend improving mechanisms for tracking these children and analyzing their performance without collecting sensitive information or endangering children and families, including creating goals and outcome measures. For example, DHS could collect and publish more-granular data on ages and most-recent known locations of children encountered at the southwest border, while NCES could collect more-detailed information on immigrants in schools by age, nationality, and year of arrival. We also recommend developing a database of types of programming offered in states, in a consistent way that enables cross-state comparisons.

Create Agreements for Educational-Record Transfers with Northern Triangle Countries

Although the United States has a memorandum of understanding with Mexico for educational records transfers for students coming from Mexico and enrolling in U.S. schools, it does not have similar agreements with Guatemala, Honduras, and El Salvador, and there are growing numbers of students from these countries in U.S. schools. Educational records are important for establishing grade-level equivalency and students' educational needs, but schools rarely have good information about the prior education of incoming undocumented and asylum-seeking children. The U.S. State Department and Department of Education should engage to develop these agreements.

Create Opportunities for Collaboration and Discussion Among the Office of Refugee Resettlement, Community Services, and Local Education Agencies

A key transition for asylum-seeking children is when they are released from ORR to a sponsor, at which point the responsibility for their education shifts to LEAs and the sponsors. For children transferred to the custody of adults who may be working long hours or away from home a lot, this is likely a moment when children fall through the cracks. ORR has case managers that confirm sponsor identities, and ORR also confirms school enrollment through a sponsor. However, a child's sponsor is the one to ensure that such children have the support they need to attend school regularly and that their nonacademic needs are met. Our interviews with policymakers and educators made clear that these children may be crossing the border with significant needs, all of which are thrown at the doorstep of schools that are typically funded just to support students' academic needs. We therefore recommend that ORR—possibly along with other federal and state agencies—work to confirm that all schools have access to willing community partners, including those that have the capacity to provide more-robust social services, medical services, and legal supports than schools are able to provide. This might take pressure off of schools to try to provide all the supports that undocumented and asylum-seeking children might need, and these supports might also benefit other children within those communities. A first step in that direction could be a set of convenings among ORR, the U.S. Department of Education and other federal agencies, SEAs and health agencies, school system administrators, and a set of robust health and community providers in areas that serve many asylum-seeking children. These convenings could cultivate a better understanding of the challenges that schools face in supporting the nonacademic needs of the students and how ORR could better connect schools with other public services to ensure that these children receive the nonacademic services they need.

Developing Policies and Processes to Address Needs of Children and Youth When They Are in K–12 Schools

Provide Additional Funding for Schools with Immigration Surges on a Rolling Basis

New students in this population arrive at schools throughout the year, with particular increases in the winter months, as shown in Chapter One. Yet schools must request funding based on student populations in August of each year, a timing that often does not align with when students arrive. This leaves schools stretched financially when they experience midyear surges in enrollment. In our interviews, school officials noted the difficulty of not being able to manage needs for recent arrivals because of this schedule. We recommend that schools have the option to request federal funding more frequently than annually, as populations change, such as quarterly.

In addition, funding is typically provided by the state to school systems based on *unduplicated counts*. Thus, a school district receives the same amount of funding for a newcomer student with low English skills and almost no formal education who is living with foster services as a newcomer student with near fluency in English and a wealthy, well-resourced family. At the least, states should consider providing additional resources to students who are from more than two disadvantaged groups, given the imbalance in instructional resources necessary for some students compared with others.

Our modeling of student populations found that school systems in seven states—as well as school systems in two counties—would have needed to hire more than 1,000 additional teachers to maintain current ratios without expanding class sizes, assuming that enrollment was otherwise unchanged. Particular attention should be focused on providing these states and counties—as well as states and counties where the recent arrivals represent large proportions of Hispanic or ELL students at baseline—with needed resources to help the newcomer populations and also to ensure that educational services are not strained for existing students. Real-time monitoring of trends at the border and in states and counties where unaccompanied children are being placed with sponsors could provide a leading indicator of near-future demands on schools.

Increase Funding and Resources for Students' Nonacademic Supports

Newly arriving undocumented and asylum-seeking children are often grappling with substantial trauma from their lives in their countries of origin, their journeys to the United States, or their current living situations. In addition to facing potential challenges to their mental health, students may be facing nonacademic challenges ranging from legal ones to physical health difficulties. These nonacademic challenges can easily spill into students' academic performance, particularly leading to higher absenteeism and eventually leading students to drop out of school entirely.

Our findings suggest a twofold problem in providing the necessary funding and resources for nonacademic supports. In Louisiana and similar states, where policies do not allow for undocumented and asylum-seeking children to receive such services as health coverage and where sanctuary policies do not offer further protection, families may be more reluctant to provide the information that schools would need to discern what supports to provide, and schools themselves may refrain from asking families what they need because of concerns about revealing their legal status. In such states, the problem is more one of helping families identify the resources they may need without identifying them as undocumented. School systems in these states would benefit from more-robust, well-resourced community networks to which they can refer needy families, as well as thoughtful approaches for schools to provide immigrant families with accessible information about those supports (e.g., videos and documents in multiple languages that introduce or catalog available resources). In contrast, in California and similar states, which are sanctuary states and provide a range of resources for undocumented children, the challenge for schools is how to make sure undocumented families are aware of all the resources available and how to access them. In these cases, well-resourced community networks are—of course—helpful, as are good and accessible sources of information on those supports. But, in addition, since schools are typically not adequately funded to provide those supports but are often called on to provide them, more school funding would enable districts to hire and train staff who can ensure that students get the services they need.

In both contexts—e.g., California and Louisiana—federal and state resources could be directed to developing stronger community networks to support students' external needs but should also be directed at providing schools with accessible documentation that they can then provide to families about those networks. In addition, more federal and state funding for the hiring and professional development of mental health and counseling services, or referrals to existing services, would expand access to much-needed counseling supports. Of course, schools are receiving additional funding relief as a result of the COVID-19 pandemic that can and should be directed toward such critical mental health supports, which will benefit immigrant and nonimmigrant students alike.

Strategically Develop, Recruit, and Place Professionals with Relevant Language and Other Needed Skills in School Districts

School districts are facing a shortage of education professionals who have the language skills and appropriate certifications to support newcomers. SEAs, postsecondary institutions, and state legislatures can collaborate to strategically develop and recruit educational professionals with relevant language and other needed skills. Creating provisions for emergency waivers or certification opportunities would expand the labor markets from which districts can recruit staff. Emergency certification opportunities may be especially important in communities that are seeing rapid growth in newcomers whose primary language is not Spanish but an indigenous language. With emergency certification or certification waiver procedures targeted to supporting undocumented and asylum-seeking children, districts may be able to develop and hire staff from the community who come with relevant language skills and a knowledge of the hardships and needs of the community.

In addition to expanding the labor pool in the short term through emergency certification and waiver processes, it would be beneficial to expand opportunities to undertake needed training and earn certifications. State agencies and postsecondary institutions can collaborate to create, expand, or tailor traditional or alternative preparation programs to broaden access to bilingual and ELL training. These efforts may require supplemental funding to implement; these efforts would be facilitated and strengthened by state legislature appropriations and targeted federal financial aid for trainees in these programs.

Another possible pathway to providing schools with the supports that they need could be the creation of a program such as AmeriCorps or alternative teacher preparation programs that provide opportunities for those with language skills to be quickly trained to provide support to English language learners. For example, after candidates receive summer training, schools could potentially hire them at a low cost to support English-language learning to teachers in classrooms and through after-school opportunities.

Relatedly, the educators in Jefferson Parish noted the effectiveness of bilingual paraprofessionals who could support ELL students in regular classrooms; a repeated wish was for more such paraprofessionals. Other districts might explore such approaches as well.

Provide Professional Learning and High-Quality Resources to All Teachers to Support English-Language Learners

Beyond ensuring that incoming staff are prepared to support ELLs, most teachers need much more training and support from school systems themselves. Our research suggests that most school systems across the United States have enrolled at least some undocumented children, and other research we have conducted suggests that nearly 40 percent of U.S. teachers, on average, teach in classrooms with at least two to three ELLs—and many more ELLs depending on where the school is located (Doan et al., 2020). As pointed out by educators and administrators in Oakland Unified, even though California teachers who work with ELLs are required to have some training in language development, teachers still often lack all the training they need to work with the range of ELLs in their classrooms.

Thus, we recommend that all teachers across the United States receive at least some training to support the language, other academic, social, and emotional growth of immigrant students, given the high likelihood that teachers will need to support at least some ELLs at some point. In states where teachers are most likely to serve ELLs, that training would be intensive, drawing on the classroom materials that teachers are expected to use in the classroom, and based on best practices for supporting the English-language development of immigrant students (e.g., National Academies of Science, Engineering, and Medicine, 2017; Weiss and Sandstead, undated).

A particular challenge for teachers is students with interrupted formal education. These students typically come into school districts without the ability to speak English proficiently and may also be several grade levels or more below their age-appropriate peers in terms of formal academic education. These students present a difficult task for educators who lack the training and resources to support them alongside all the other students in the educators' regular classrooms. Even in our case study school systems, where there are thoughtful, long-term programs for supporting newcomers to the United States, teachers struggled to serve such students, which suggests that in districts without such programs, these students are likely floundering or falling through the cracks, which may especially be the case during the COVID-19 pandemic (Chang-Bacon, 2021).

Several educators with whom we spoke in our case study school systems pointed directly to resources provided by the New York State Department of Education to support students with interrupted formal education, which these educators wished would be available in their state (New York State Department of Education, 2021). These challenges point to the need for many more opportunities for collaboration among schools and educators serving students with interrupted formal education, as well as repositories and one-stop shops for materials and training to support these populations. As demonstrated by the New York State Department of Education, SEAs are a logical group to bring educators together within states, but SEAs likely need federal funding and support to do so.

Furthermore, educators in Louisiana noted significant needs for Spanish-language tests that could help in grade placement. Such tests should be available for schools nationally to use as a resource for grade placement. One option would be for the U.S. Department of Education to develop a general set of materials that could be used as resources by districts around the country.

Provide Information and Training for All School System Staff Who Engage with Undocumented and Asylum-Seeking Children

Beyond providing teachers with the professional development they need to support students' English-language learning and nonacademic supports, all school system staff—including administrators, any instructional staff, and noninstructional staff from school secretaries to perhaps even bus drivers—should possess a thorough and up-to-date understanding of the responsibilities of the school and district to enroll and provide a quality education for newcomer children, as well as the immigration policies that may affect children's school experiences. Increasing collaboration between SEAs, the U.S. Department of Education, districts, and educator training programs may help fill some these gaps in knowledge. Education agencies at the state and federal levels already offer many resources and opportunities for engagement and clarification to school staff of their responsibilities and roles in supporting undocumented and asylum-seeking students. The dissemination of accessible, quick-reference-style information and resources to leadership in districts, instructors in educator training programs, and all incoming school staff would continue to facilitate the rooting out of misinformation and the building of practice that is consistent with policy. For instance, the incorporation of a session or unit covering immigration law, the educational rights of undocumented and asylum-seeking children, and the newcomer enrollment process during district onboarding for new front-line staff or in educator training programs has the potential to ensure policy-aligned practices for all new staff and educators.

Create More-Targeted Career and Technical Education Approaches

A key challenge in both case study school districts was in preparing high school ELL students who were academically behind for the workforce after high school. Challenges included lacking targeted skill programs relevant to the types of jobs available in the labor market; the need to integrate English-language, relevant math, and technical skills into single courses; requirements for Social Security numbers for minors to take certain certification tests; and the lack of high school graduation pathways for students with interrupted formal education. The U.S. Department of Education and SEAs should develop federal or state guidance regarding secondary training opportunities.

Improve the Evidence Base About Critical Underresearched Areas

Our work has filled some of the gaps in knowledge and evidence about undocumented and asylum-seeking children. However, the evidence base must be improved even further to support the education of undocumented and asylum-seeking children, given the additional gaps uncovered by our research. Such areas include the following (some of which are also part of previous recommendations in this chapter):

- data on where such students are, as well as their needs, including any such data being compiled by individual school districts and used to support planning and decisionmaking (we have used models to estimate this information, but better data collection could improve the data and models we have identified)
- cross-state comparisons on the efficacy of programming for ELLs, to better understand the diversity of ELL needs and assets (this should include data on the demographics of students—such as newcomers, ELLs born in the United States, and needs of students with different language backgrounds)
- data about perspectives of teachers with newcomers, ELLs, and students with interrupted formal education in their mainstream classrooms, including benefits, challenges, useful approaches, and gaps, along with classroom observations, to better support and prepare these teachers
- perspectives of newcomer parents and children about their educational experiences and needs
- better approaches for the education of students with interrupted formal education

- curricula and interventions that support ELLs in learning English while also providing access to rigorous academic content
- approaches in communities that are able to partner with schools and provide nonacademic services to undocumented children
- challenges related to children's transitions from CBP to ORR and ORR to local communities
- training pipelines and labor markets for teachers and staff with critically needed language, instructional, and counseling skills
- increasing attendance and retention through to graduation
- improved connections with postsecondary work and education opportunities.

Modeling Approach and Data Tables

We drew on a range of data sources to estimate the number of recently arrived undocumented and asylum-seeking children, the distribution of these children across states and counties, and children's impact on school systems. In doing so, we made several simplifying assumptions, a necessity given that neither timely, cross-sectional data identifying individuals as undocumented or asylum-seeking migrants nor comprehensive, longitudinal data that track children and families across various touchpoints with federal agencies *and to specific locations and ultimately schools* are available.

Our methodological approach consisted of four key steps:

1. Estimate the total number of recently arrived undocumented and asylum-seeking children in the country.
2. Estimate the age distribution of these children and the share who are enrolled in school.
3. Estimate the distribution of these children across states and counties.
4. Estimate the impact of these children on state and county school systems by scaling the estimates to education indicators of interest.

In Chapter Two, we described how we drew on DHS data newly made available in December 2020 in the *Fiscal Year 2020 Enforcement Lifecycle Report* (Rosenblum and Zhang, 2020) to estimate that 491,200 children from Mexico and the Northern Triangle countries arrived over fiscal years 2017 through 2019 (i.e., from October 2016 to September 2019) and remained in the country in undocumented status as of March 2020. Although we made several assumptions (described in the chapter) to estimate *children* remaining in the country in unresolved status,[1] these counts largely reflect the assumptions and limitations of the underlying DHS data—for example, the assumption that *no confirmed departure* is equivalent to *did not depart*.

In the sections below, we describe steps 2 through 4 of our modeling approach in greater detail, enumerating our data sources and assumptions, and presenting additional data on states and counties outside the top ten presented in the body of the report.

---

[1] Specifically, we assumed that 54 percent of encounters of family units from the Northern Triangle and 56 percent of encounters of family units from Mexico were children. Additionally, we assumed that the distribution of statuses as of March 2020 was equivalent for children in family units as for family units overall.

Age Distribution of Recent Arrivals and Share Enrolled in School

Of the 491,200 undocumented and asylum-seeking children from Mexico and the Northern Triangle countries who were under age 18 upon arrival in FYs 2017–2019 and in the United States in March 2020, some were not yet elementary-school age, while others were 18 or older and more likely to be in the workforce or possibly postsecondary school than in K–12 education systems. Moreover, some children of elementary- or secondary-school age do not attend school, despite their right under *Plyler v. Doe* to do so, for reasons that may include prioritizing work over school, fear of coming out of the shadows and engaging with formal public sector systems in any capacity, or complexities or burdens imposed in particular states or localities that make it difficult to enroll.

Figure A.1 displays our approach for estimating the number of recent arrivals in schools. We make these calculations separately for arrivals from Mexico and the Northern Triangle countries and for unaccompanied children and children in family units. In doing so, we draw on CBP data made available by TRAC, which parses apprehension data into individual ages in addition to by nationality and category of child (TRAC Reports, undated-a).

As described in Chapter Two, we estimate that about 321,000 individuals from Mexico and the Northern Triangle countries who arrived as children over FYs 2017–2019 remained in the United States in unresolved status and attended primary or secondary schools in March 2020—i.e., during the 2019–2020 school year. This represents a little under two-thirds (65 percent) of the number of these child arrivals we estimate to be in the country and about 56 percent of the roughly 574,000 CBP encounters of children from these countries over the fiscal years of interest.

With respect to the age distribution upon arrival, we found little variation by nationality within categories (i.e., unaccompanied children versus children in family units) but sharp differences between these two categories of children. Most unaccompanied children are in their teens when they arrive, while most children in family units are age 12 and under.

FIGURE A.1

Estimation Approach for the Number of Recently Arrived Undocumented and Asylum-Seeking Children in School

NOTE: Estimated separately for Mexico and the Northern Triangle and by category of child (unaccompanied child or child in family unit), and then summed.

We make several simplifying assumptions to estimate the age distribution of recent arrivals who remain in the United States. These are listed in Table A.1. Our assumptions regarding the share of children in schools by age group (listed in Table 2.3) are derived from aggregate data on the share of unauthorized (i.e., undocumented and asylum-seeking) children in school published by the Migration Policy Institute.[2] The Migration Policy Institute data suggest that most K–12 school-age undocumented and asylum-seeking children do attend school, albeit at a somewhat lower rate than NCES data show for the overall population of children (NCES, 2018). Compulsory education laws across the states lend support to our

TABLE A.1

Assumptions Made in Estimating Age Distribution

Category	Assumptions
Age distribution of *arriving* children	We include all available years of apprehension data from TRAC, FYs 2015–2018, in estimating the age distribution for each nationality category of child group and apply these shares to all years in our data. Hence, we do not capture any changes in the age distribution within groups over time.[a]
	We assume that the age distribution of all southwest border encounters (including apprehensions and inadmissibles) for each nationality category group matches the distribution for that group based on the TRAC apprehensions data.
Age distribution of children *remaining* in the United States in unresolved status	We age the children forward one to three years, depending on when they arrived, to estimate the *March 2020* age distribution of recent arrivals. For example, for arrivals in FY 2017, we age them forward three years such that the estimated number of 17-year-olds upon arrival is the estimated number of 20-year-olds in March 2020. For arrivals in FY 2018, we age them forward two years such that a 17-year-old upon arrival is 19 years old. We age arrivals in FY 2019 forward one year such that 17-year-olds are considered to be 18-year-olds.
	We assume that there is no variation by age within nationality category groups in the individuals' statuses as of March 2020—i.e., in the share remaining in the country in unresolved status.
	For the purposes of estimating the distribution of the children across states and counties (described later in this section), we assume that the age distribution by nationality does not vary by geography.

[a] Data from ORR on the age distribution of unaccompanied children (of all countries of origin) by fiscal year over the FYs 2015–2019 period show little variation over time (ORR, 2021).

---

[2]   We note that the Migration Policy Institute's age groupings do not align with ours, nor are they restricted to recent arrivals from Mexico and the Northern Triangle. Recent arrivals may be less likely to attend school than children who have been in the United States for longer. Also, note that the Migration Policy Institute refers to this group as "unauthorized" (Gelatt and Zong, 2018).

assumption that most children who reach elementary-school age but remain under 18 attend school (NCES, undated-c).

Distribution Across States and Counties

To better understand the localized impacts of recently arrived children on school systems, we estimated the distribution of these children across the country at the state and county levels. In doing so, we drew on three separate data sources, two of which included data at the county level and all three of which included data for states.

Both state- and county-level data were available for what we refer to as the *baseline* distribution of these children, reflecting the distribution of undocumented and asylum-seeking immigrants from Mexico and Central America over the 2012–2016 period, on average, as estimated by the Migration Policy Institute.[3] Data at both levels were also available from the HHS ORR for geography, with a breakdown of where unaccompanied children are released to sponsors, by fiscal year, albeit without parsing by country of origin for these children. Last, for the state distribution only, we utilized data from TRAC on the location of the immigration courts where juvenile cases were initiated in recent fiscal years for children from Mexico and each of the Northern Triangle countries.

These three data sources each have strengths and weaknesses, providing some signal of where recently arrived children are located but with variation in the coverage, granularity, and vintage of the data. Hence, in making our estimates, we weighted the sources equally, basing one-third of our estimate on each of the three sources for our state-level estimates and half on each of the two sources with county-level data for our county-level estimates. Figure A.2 displays our weighting procedure at the state level, calculated separately for children from Mexico and the Northern Triangle. Our county-level estimation approach is similar, weighting the first two sources equally. Below, we describe the three data sources that factor into our weighted estimates, our weighting procedure, and the limitations of our estimation approach.

Baseline (2012–2016) Distribution of Undocumented and Asylum-Seeking Immigrants

We expect that the distribution of where undocumented immigrants and asylum-seekers from Mexico and the Northern Triangle countries have lived in the past provides a useful signal of where recently arrived children settle. Because regular Census Bureau surveys, such

---

[3] The Migration Policy Institute provided RAND with estimates of the number of *unauthorized* (the term the Migration Policy Institute uses) immigrants from Mexico and Central America by state and for the top 50 counties (by overall unauthorized population). These tabulations were based on the institute's work to estimate the unauthorized population using 2012–2016 five-year averages from the Census Bureau's American Community Survey, along with various characteristics of this population (see Gelatt and Zong, 2018).

FIGURE A.2

Estimation Approach for the Distribution of Recently Arrived Undocumented and Asylum-Seeking Children Across States

NOTES: Estimated separately for Mexico and the Northern Triangle, reflecting the granularity with which the Migration Policy Institute and EOIR data from TRAC are available. Baseline estimates for the Northern Triangle reflect the distribution of unauthorized immigrants from Central America overall. Unaccompanied children data are inclusive of unaccompanied children of all countries of origin.

as the Decennial Census and the American Community Survey, do not ask respondents to identify their legal status (though they do ask about place of birth, and the American Community Survey asks about citizenship), researchers have developed methods to estimate the size and characteristics of this population. Most common are *residual-based* methods that use various data sources to estimate the size of the legal immigrant population and assume that the residual between this estimate and the total foreign-born population consists of immigrants without legal status (Baker, 2018; Capps et al., 2020; Passel and Cohn, 2018; Warren, 2021). These methods may be paired with imputation methods that draw on past Census Bureau surveys that did ask noncitizens whether they had lawful permanent resident status (Gelatt and Zong, 2018).

The Migration Policy Institute provided us with the data we used to establish our baseline distribution. The data we received included detailed tabulations derived from the institute's prior work to estimate the size and characteristics of the unauthorized (i.e., undocumented and asylum-seeking) population using 2012–2016 averages from the American Community Survey.[4] We received data for 41 states and the District and Columbia, as well as for the top 50 counties by overall unauthorized population. Sample sizes were inadequate for the remaining states and counties to support reliable estimation. The data were parsed by age (0–17 and 18 and older) and by region of birth, with categories for Mexico and Central America. We made a simplifying assumption that the distribution for the Northern Triangle countries was consistent with the distribution for Central America overall. We further assumed that the overall distribution (including adults and children) was equivalent to the distribution of children, in light of very small sample sizes for children from Central America in particular,

---

[4] Migration Policy Institute analysis of U.S. Census Bureau data from the pooled Census Bureau's 2012–2016 American Community Survey and the 2008 Survey of Income and Program Participation, drawing on a methodology developed in consultation with James Bachmeier of Temple University and Jennifer Van Hook of Pennsylvania State University, Population Research Institute. See Gelatt and Zong, 2018.

which precluded us from estimating the county-level distribution of these children for all but 11 counties for which we received data.

After employing our assumption that the distribution of children matches the distribution of all of these immigrants, the Migration Policy Institute estimates suggest that 85 percent of children from Central America were in 13 states—with California, Texas, Florida, New York, Maryland, Virginia, and New Jersey each home to at least 5 percent. California and Texas alone accounted for about one-third of these children. With respect to Mexican children, the Migration Policy Institute estimates suggest that nearly 55 percent were in those same two states—California and Texas—and that Illinois was the only other state home to at least 5 percent of this population.

At the county level, the 50 counties for which we received data from the Migration Policy Institute accounted for 63 percent all of these immigrants from Central America and 56 percent from Mexico. We do not attempt to allocate the portions of the distribution that are not allocated by the Migration Policy Institute, meaning that our final estimates by county may underestimate the population of recently arrived children for counties with insufficient sample sizes to be estimated by the Migration Policy Institute.

Unaccompanied Children Released to Sponsors, FYs 2017–2019

When CBP encounters unaccompanied children from noncontiguous countries (and a portion from Mexico) are encountered, they are transferred to the custody of ORR, which is required to ensure that unaccompanied children "be promptly placed in the least restrictive setting that is in the best interest of the child" while awaiting their immigration hearings (8 U.S.C. 1232[c][2][A]). ORR reports data, by fiscal year, on the locations where unaccompanied children are released to sponsors, for all states and for counties where at least 50 unaccompanied children in a given fiscal year are placed with sponsors (Administration for Children and Families, 2021a, 2021b). We use the state- and county-level distributions in the ORR data as a second signal of where recently arrived children are located, with this source contributing one-third to the weighted state estimates and one-half to the weighted county estimates.[5]

Using the ORR data, summing over FYs 2017–2019, we are able to allocate the entirety of the distribution to the states and about 80 percent to the counties (the remainder reflecting counties that never received 50 or more unaccompanied child placements in a fiscal year). Although all states received unaccompanied-child placements over these three years, more than half were in just five states—Texas, California, Florida, New York, and Maryland.

---

[5] Because more than 90 percent of unaccompanied children who have passed through ORR in recent years are from El Salvador, Guatemala, or Honduras, we assume that the distribution of unaccompanied children released to sponsors over FYs 2017–2019 reflects the distribution of where children from the Northern Triangle are placed, despite the data not parsing by country of origin. Moreover, though it is not inclusive of children in family units, we assume that the ORR released-to-sponsors distribution reasonably reflects the communities where these children may locate. We note that this source is likely less representative of where children from Mexico settle (ORR, 2021).

Roughly another quarter were in six more states—Virginia, New Jersey, Georgia, North Carolina, Tennessee, and Louisiana. At the county level, 229 counties appear in the data, though the top 15 counties accounted for about one-third of the placements and the top 40 accounted for a majority.

Juvenile Executive Office of Immigration Review Removal Proceedings Initiated, FYs 2018–2019

The final source contributing to our estimates of the distribution of recently arrived children is the EOIR data on juvenile proceedings made available by TRAC (TRAC Reports, undated-b).[6] These data list the state where the immigration court to which a case is assigned is located, in addition to the country of origin for the child and the fiscal year of initiation for the case. We use these court locations as a third signal of where the children are living across the states and generate separate distributions for children from the Northern Triangle countries (summing El Salvador, Guatemala, and Honduras) and Mexico.[7] These data are not available by county.

The distributions of children across the states calculated using this method are skewed in a similar fashion as the Migration Policy Institute– and ORR-based distributions (i.e., a small number of states accounts for a large majority of the children). Ten states account for 75 percent of the case distribution for the Northern Triangle: Texas, California, Florida, New York, Virginia, Georgia, North Carolina, Louisiana, Tennessee, and Maryland. The top ten states account for about 78 percent of the distribution of juvenile cases for Mexican nationals: Texas, California, Georgia, Arizona, Louisiana, Washington, Florida, Illinois, Colorado, and Nevada.

Weighted Distribution

There is a great deal of consistency in the distributions derived using the three methods. Nonetheless, recognizing that each method reflected a different approach to signaling where recent arrivals are located, we weight the sources equally in deriving our final estimates.

In calculating the weighted distribution, we assume that counties with insufficient sample sizes and for which we did not receive data from the Migration Policy Institute and counties never receiving at least 50 unaccompanied children in a fiscal year are zeros. Ultimately,

---

[6] We summed data for cases initiated in FYs 2018–2019, when the data are inclusive of all juvenile cases, and excluded FY 2017–initiated cases, which included only unaccompanied children. The rationale for this approach is that, because data on unaccompanied children released to sponsors contribute one-third to the weighted distribution across states, the one-third weight derived from the EOIR data should not unnecessarily lean further in the direction of reflecting where unaccompanied children are located.

[7] We note that according to DHS's *Fiscal Year 2020 Enforcement Lifecycle Report* (Rosenblum and Zhang, 2020), only a portion of children encountered over FYs 2017 through 2019 with unresolved status and no confirmed departure are in EOIR proceedings, with another portion being processed by DHS. The case distribution by state may be less representative for migrants who are not in EOIR proceedings.

this results in our leaving about 38 percent of the weighted distribution of children from the Northern Triangle across the counties unallocated and about 42 percent of the county-level distribution of children from Mexico unallocated. As noted, this means that we likely are underestimating the share of children in a portion of counties for which we do not have complete data.

Inevitably, our estimated distribution might not match the actual distribution of recently arrived undocumented and asylum-seeking children from Mexico and the Northern Triangle. This is both because of limitations in measuring the data we use to derive our estimates (e.g., insufficient sample size) and because none of these measurements was designed to capture precisely what we are seeking to estimate. For example, the baseline distribution might not reflect where new arrivals settle, that unaccompanied children may move from where they are initially placed with sponsors, and that children may settle in states other than where their court cases are. However, we believe that, collectively, these various sources provide us with a reasonable estimate of where recent arrivals are living and where the impacts on local school systems are concentrated.

Impact on State and County School Systems

The final step in our modeling process is to scale our estimates of the number of recently arrived undocumented and asylum-seeking children in primary and secondary school systems in states and counties across the country to education indicators of interest. We take this step to provide context for the raw numbers and highlight the localized impacts of these recent arrivals. For example, the same numerical increase may affect areas very differently depending on their size, available resources, and experience educating students with similar characteristics as the recent arrivals. Here, we describe our data and methods for estimating the impacts on state and county school systems and then present detailed data tables at the state and county levels.

Data and Methods

We draw on data from the NCES Common Core of Data program, which annually collects information from public school districts across the country, as aggregated in NCES's Elementary and Secondary Information System (ElSi) (NCES, undated-d). For states, we download data on the number of students in public elementary and secondary schools, as well as the number of students in the following groups into which newly arriving children from the Northern Triangle likely fit: Hispanic students, LEP or ELL students, and students receiving FRL (a proxy for low-income students).

The state data also include counts of the number of full-time-equivalent teachers and school staff overall, consisting of administrators, guidance counselors, instructional aides, librarians, and other support staff.[8] We use these data to estimate the number of additional teachers and other staff that would be needed to educate the recent arrivals while holding baseline student-teacher and student-staff ratios constant. Specifically, to make these calculations, we calculate the number of teachers and other staff (i.e., overall staff subtracting out teachers) per enrolled pupil in the baseline school year (e.g., 15 students per teacher). We then divide our estimate of recent arrivals by these values to determine the number of additional personnel needed, assuming enrollment was otherwise unchanged (e.g., 15,000 additional students divided by 15 results in an estimate of 1,000 additional teachers needed to hold constant the baseline 15–1 student-teacher ratio).

We download the same data elements for counties, although county data are unavailable for the share of LEP or ELL students and are available only for full-time-equivalent teachers and not for school staff overall. For both states and counties, we use data from the 2016–2017 school year as our baseline prior to the arrival of these children over FYs 2017 through 2019. We list the assumptions and limitations associated with our data and methods for scaling to education indicators in Table A.2.

Although the state and in particular county levels of analysis seek to present localized impacts of recent arrivals, ultimately the impacts may be more localized than we are able to estimate. For example, in some cases public school systems align with county borders, but in

TABLE A.2

Assumptions Made in Scaling Estimates to Education Indicators

Assumption	Implication
Recent arrivals enroll in public schools rather than private schools	If any recent arrivals enroll in private schools, our estimates would overstate recent arrivals as a share of public school enrollments
The size of the enrolled population at public schools otherwise would have held steady	Offsetting flows of students and unrelated changes to enrollments are not accounted for in the estimates, whether of undocumented and asylum-seeking children who had been in the state or county public school systems at baseline or other categories of children
Recent arrivals enrolling in public schools were from the Northern Triangle countries or Mexico	Recent arrivals from other countries of origin are not included in our estimates
All recent arrivals are Hispanic, ELL or LEP, and qualify for FRL	If recent arrivals are not in these categories, we would overstate the percentage impact for students in those groups
Arrivals prior to FY 2017 were enrolled in the schools during the baseline period, and arrivals in FY 2017 did not enroll until at least the 2017–2018 school year	Arrivals prior to FY 2017 who enrolled in the 2017–2018 school year or later contribute neither to the baseline estimate nor to our estimate new enrollees, while arrivals in FY 2017 who enrolled in 2016–2017 would be double-counted in the baseline and the estimate of new enrollees

---

[8] For a full list of positions included in the overall staff measure, see ED*Facts* Submission System, 2017.

other cases there are multiple school districts in a county. Inevitably, some districts in these counties see larger impacts than others.

Detailed Data Tables

In Chapter Two, we presented information on the top ten states and counties by total estimated number of recently arrived undocumented and asylum-seeking children from Mexico and the Northern Triangle. Tables A.3 and A.4 provide additional details on the distribution of these children across states and counties, respectively, and the relative impacts on school systems for all states and counties that we estimate were home to at least 1,000 recently arrived children as of March 2020.

The detailed data tables underscore that states and counties with the largest impacts in raw numerical terms might not be the ones with the largest impacts relative to baseline populations of Hispanic, ELL or LEP, and FRL students, and vice versa. For example, although California, Texas, Florida, and New York top the list in terms of the most recent arrivals—and counties in these states are included among the top ten counties by count—their large Hispanic student populations at baseline result in them not being among the top states in terms of relative impacts. Conversely, in 14 counties not in the top ten in terms of the estimated number of recent arrivals, the recent arrivals are more than 5 percent of the baseline Hispanic student population, including counties in California, Connecticut, Georgia, Louisiana, Maryland, Massachusetts, New Jersey, North Carolina, and Tennessee.

Counts and relative shares provide complementary information and each capture a portion of the anticipated impacts on states and counties. Counts offer a simple means to compare where recent arrivals are located and sheds light on where the newcomer population is large enough in magnitude to potentially rise on the agenda of planners and policymakers. However, in the case of large states with large baseline populations of similar students, including earlier cohorts of undocumented and asylum-seeking students, simply receiving a larger number of newcomers than other, smaller states does not necessarily mean that impacts are concentrated there. A focus on relative shares shifts the emphasis to locations that may be smaller in size but where the impact of the newcomers may be felt more intensively. However, in the case of smaller states with smaller numbers of newcomers, the limitations of our methods may be more acute and more affected by shifts over time in where newcomers locate. For example, although it would take large changes in location patterns to meaningfully alter the impacts on larger states and counties, smaller shifts could meaningfully change the picture for less populous areas.

TABLE A.3

Estimated State-Level Impacts of Recently Arrived Undocumented Immigrant and Asylum-Seeking Children from Mexico and the Northern Triangle on Primary- and Secondary-School Systems, as of March 2020—States with 1,000 or More Recent Arrivals

State	Number of Children in School	Share of Recent Arrivals	Share of Baseline Students, Overall	Share of Baseline Students, Hispanic	Share of Baseline Students, LEP or ELL	Share of Baseline Students, FRL	Additional Teachers Needed	Additional Other Staff Needed
California	51,600	16.1%	0.8%	1.5%	4.1%	1.4%	2,250	2,720
Texas	48,200	15.0%	0.9%	1.7%	5.2%	1.5%	3,170	3,180
Florida	29,900	9.3%	1.1%	3.3%	10.4%	1.8%	1,980	1,760
New York	23,800	7.4%	0.9%	3.3%	—	1.7%	1,820	1,550
Virginia	18,500	5.8%	1.4%	9.5%	18.3%	3.5%	1,310	1,270
Maryland	16,900	5.3%	1.9%	11.6%	24.5%	4.1%	1,140	1,110
New Jersey	14,700	4.6%	1.0%	3.8%	—	2.8%	1,210	1,270
Georgia	13,600	4.2%	0.8%	5.1%	11.9%	1.2%	880	880
North Carolina	12,900	4.0%	0.8%	4.9%	13.9%	1.4%	830	770
Louisiana	9,200	2.9%	1.3%	20.2%	—	2.0%	620	630
Tennessee	9,000	2.8%	0.9%	9.3%	20.9%	—	580	580
Massachusetts	6,800	2.1%	0.7%	3.7%	7.9%	—	510	410
Illinois	5,300	1.6%	0.3%	1.0%	—	0.5%	340	340
Pennsylvania	5,300	1.6%	0.3%	2.8%	—	0.7%	370	380
Ohio	3,900	1.2%	0.2%	4.2%	—	—	230	500
Arizona	3,600	1.1%	0.3%	0.7%	—	—	150	180
Colorado	3,600	1.1%	0.4%	1.2%	3.4%	1.0%	210	240
Washington	3,600	1.1%	0.3%	1.4%	—	0.8%	190	120
Missouri	3,300	1.0%	0.4%	5.8%	—	0.7%	250	200

Table A.3—Continued

State	Number of Children in School	Share of Recent Arrivals	Share of Baseline Students, Overall	Share of Baseline Students, Hispanic	Share of Baseline Students, LEP or ELL	Share of Baseline Students, FRL	Additional Teachers Needed	Additional Other Staff Needed
Nebraska	3,200	1.0%	1.0%	5.3%	—	2.2%	230	240
Connecticut	3,100	1.0%	0.6%	2.4%	8.6%	1.7%	250	310
Minnesota	3,100	1.0%	0.4%	3.9%	—	0.9%	200	220
Kentucky	2,700	0.8%	0.4%	6.1%	12.1%	0.7%	160	220
Alabama	2,500	0.8%	0.3%	4.4%	11.9%	0.6%	140	150
Nevada	2,400	0.8%	0.5%	1.2%	3.2%	0.8%	120	60
South Carolina	2,300	0.7%	0.3%	3.4%	5.3%	0.5%	150	110
Indiana	1,700	0.5%	0.2%	1.4%	3.6%	0.3%	100	140
Oregon	1,700	0.5%	0.3%	1.3%	—	0.6%	90	110
Michigan	1,500	0.5%	0.1%	1.3%	—	0.2%	80	100
Arkansas	1,400	0.4%	0.3%	2.2%	—	0.8%	100	110
Oklahoma	1,400	0.4%	0.2%	1.2%	—	0.3%	80	90
District of Columbia	1,200	0.4%	1.4%	8.8%	—	—	90	90
Kansas	1,200	0.4%	0.2%	1.3%	—	0.5%	90	80
Rhode Island	1,200	0.4%	0.8%	3.4%	10.9%	1.8%	90	80
Utah	1,200	0.4%	0.2%	1.1%	—	0.5%	50	60
Iowa	1,000	0.3%	0.2%	1.9%	—	0.5%	70	80
Mississippi	1,000	0.3%	0.2%	5.7%	7.5%	0.3%	70	70

SOURCES: Authors' estimates based on data from DHS, TRAC Reports, MPI, ORR, and NCES.

NOTES: — = missing in underlying data source. "Number of Newcomer Children in School" is the estimated number of recently arrived undocumented and asylum-seeking children in schools (rounded to the nearest hundred). "Share of Recent Arrivals" is the share of the total estimate of 321,000 arrivals nationwide in the state (derived from unrounded numbers). "Share of Baseline Students" columns indicate these arrivals as a share of baseline public school enrollment in the state, specifically of overall enrollment, Hispanic enrollment, LEP or ELL enrollment, and FRL enrollment. The estimated numbers of additional teachers and additional other staff needed to accommodate these arrivals (rounded to the nearest ten) reflect the numbers of these personnel needed to maintain baseline student–teacher and student–overall staff ratios, assuming that the enrolled population otherwise would have held steady.

TABLE A.4

Estimated County-Level Impacts of Recently Arrived Undocumented and Asylum-Seeking Children from Mexico and the Northern Triangle on Primary- and Secondary-School Systems, as of December 2019—Top 50 Counties by Estimated Number of Children

County	State	Number of Children in School	Share of Recent Arrivals	Share of Baseline Students, Overall	Share of Baseline Students, Hispanic	Share of Baseline Students, FRL	Additional Teachers Needed
Los Angeles County	California	30,400	9.5%	2.0%	3.1%	3.0%	1,300
Harris County	Texas	19,900	6.2%	2.2%	3.9%	3.4%	1,220
Miami-Dade County	Florida	9,300	2.9%	2.6%	3.7%	3.7%	530
Prince George's County	Maryland	7,600	2.4%	5.8%	18.6%	8.6%	520
Dallas County	Texas	6,600	2.1%	1.3%	2.4%	1.8%	420
Suffolk County	New York	6,200	1.9%	2.6%	8.9%	6.9%	440
Montgomery County	Maryland	6,100	1.9%	3.8%	12.8%	11.0%	400
Fairfax County	Virginia	6,100	1.9%	3.4%	13.3%	12.5%	410
Palm Beach County	Florida	5,900	1.8%	3.0%	9.1%	5.2%	400
Nassau County	New York	5,000	1.5%	2.4%	9.9%	8.6%	380
Suffolk County	Massachusetts	4,500	1.4%	5.4%	12.2%	—	320
Queens County	New York	4,300	1.3%	1.5%	3.9%	2.2%	280
Union County	New Jersey	3,600	1.1%	3.8%	9.7%	8.2%	290
Alameda County	California	3,300	1.0%	1.4%	4.3%	3.4%	150
Broward County	Florida	3,300	1.0%	1.2%	3.6%	1.9%	190
Kings County	New York	3,200	1.0%	1.0%	3.6%	1.4%	230

Table A.4—Continued

County	State	Number of Children in School	Share of Recent Arrivals	Share of Baseline Students, Overall	Share of Baseline Students, Hispanic	Share of Baseline Students, FRL	Additional Teachers Needed
Mecklenburg County	North Carolina	3,200	1.0%	2.0%	9.1%	3.4%	190
Hudson County	New Jersey	3,000	0.9%	3.4%	5.8%	4.9%	230
Orange County	California	2,800	0.9%	0.6%	1.1%	1.2%	110
Fairfield County	Connecticut	2,600	0.8%	1.8%	6.7%	5.9%	190
Travis County	Texas	2,500	0.8%	1.3%	2.6%	2.7%	170
Riverside County	California	2,300	0.7%	0.5%	0.9%	0.9%	100
Cook County	Illinois	2,300	0.7%	0.3%	0.8%	0.5%	140
Gwinnett County	Georgia	2,200	0.7%	1.2%	4.0%	2.2%	140
San Mateo County	California	2,100	0.7%	2.2%	5.8%	6.9%	100
Maricopa County	Arizona	2,000	0.6%	0.3%	0.6%	—	80
Clark County	Nevada	2,000	0.6%	0.6%	1.3%	0.9%	100
San Bernardino County	California	2,000	0.6%	0.5%	0.8%	0.7%	80
Essex County	New Jersey	1,900	0.6%	1.4%	5.5%	2.7%	150
Bronx County	New York	1,900	0.6%	0.8%	1.4%	1.0%	140
Westchester County	New York	1,900	0.6%	1.3%	4.0%	3.5%	140
Contra Costa County	California	1,800	0.6%	1.0%	2.9%	2.6%	80
Orange County	Florida	1,700	0.5%	0.8%	2.1%	1.2%	110
Bergen County	New Jersey	1,700	0.5%	1.2%	5.0%	5.8%	140

Table A.4—Continued

County	State	Number of Children in School	Share of Recent Arrivals	Share of Baseline Students, Overall	Share of Baseline Students, Hispanic	Share of Baseline Students, FRL	Additional Teachers Needed
Tarrant County	Texas	1,700	0.5%	0.4%	1.1%	0.8%	110
Santa Clara County	California	1,700	0.5%	0.6%	1.6%	1.7%	70
Lee County	Florida	1,600	0.5%	1.7%	4.4%	3.3%	100
Davidson County	Tennessee	1,600	0.5%	1.8%	8.0%	—	90
San Diego County	California	1,500	0.5%	0.3%	0.6%	0.6%	60
Jefferson Parish	Louisiana	1,400	0.4%	2.8%	10.7%	4.4%	80
King County	Washington	1,300	0.4%	0.5%	2.6%	1.3%	70
Baltimore city	Maryland	1,200	0.4%	1.5%	15.6%	1.5%	70
DeKalb County	Georgia	1,200	0.4%	1.0%	6.4%	1.5%	80
Bexar County	Texas	1,200	0.4%	0.3%	0.5%	0.5%	80
Prince William County	Virginia	1,100	0.3%	1.2%	3.7%	3.1%	70
Mercer County	New Jersey	1,100	0.3%	1.9%	7.6%	4.7%	90
Fresno County	California	1,100	0.4%	0.6%	0.9%	0.8%	50
Middlesex County	New Jersey	1,100	0.3%	0.8%	2.9%	2.4%	90
Baltimore County	Maryland	1,000	0.3%	0.9%	10.0%	1.9%	60
Essex County	Massachusetts	1,000	0.3%	0.9%	2.6%	—	80

SOURCES: Authors' estimates based on data from DHS, TRAC Reports, MPI, ORR, and NCES.

NOTES: — = missing in underlying data source; "Number of Newcomer Children in School" is the estimated number of recently arrived undocumented and asylum-seeking children in schools (rounded to the nearest hundred). "Share of Recent Arrivals" is the share of the total estimate of 321,000 arrivals nationwide in the county (derived from unrounded numbers). "Share of Baseline Students" columns indicate these arrivals as a share of baseline public school enrollment in the state, specifically of overall enrollment, Hispanic enrollment, and FRL enrollment. The estimated numbers of additional teachers needed to accommodate these arrivals (rounded to the nearest ten) reflect the number needed to maintain baseline student-teacher ratios assuming that the enrolled population otherwise would have held steady.

Abbreviations

CBP	U.S. Customs and Border Protection
DACA	Deferred Action for Childhood Arrivals
DAPA	Deferred Action for Parents of Americans and Lawful Permanent Residents
DHS	U.S. Department of Homeland Security
DOJ	U.S. Department of Justice
ELL	English-language learner
EOIR	Executive Office of Immigration Review
ESL	English as a second language
ESSA	Every Student Succeeds Act
FRL	free or reduced-price lunches
FY	fiscal year
HHS	U.S. Department of Health and Human Services
ICE	U.S. Immigration and Customs Enforcement
LEA	local education agency
LEP	limited English proficiency
MPP	Migrant Protection Protocols
NCES	National Center for Education Statistics
ORR	Office of Refugee Resettlement
SEA	state education agency
TRAC	Transactional Records Access Clearinghouse

References

Administration for Children and Families, U.S. Department of Health and Human Services, "Unaccompanied Children Released to Sponsors by State—September 2019," last reviewed March 24, 2021a. As of April 2, 2021:
https://www.hhs.gov/programs/social-services/unaccompanied-children-released-to-sponsors-by-county-september-2019.html

———, "Unaccompanied Children Released to Sponsors by State—November 2019," last reviewed, March 24, 2021b. As of April 2, 2021:
https://www.hhs.gov/programs/social-services/unaccompanied-children-released-to-sponsors-by-state-november-2019.html

Amadeo, Kimberly, "Donald Trump on Immigration: The Economic Impact of Trump's Immigration Policies," *The Balance*, updated February 23, 2021. As of April 2, 2021:
https://www.thebalance.com/donald-trump-immigration-impact-on-economy-4151107

American Immigration Council, "Policies Affecting Asylum Seekers at the Border: The Migrant Protection Protocols, Prompt Asylum Claim Review, Humanitarian Asylum Review Process, Metering, Asylum Transit Ban, and How They Interact," fact sheet, January 29, 2020. As of April 2, 2021:
https://www.americanimmigrationcouncil.org/research/policies-affecting-asylum-seekers-border

Annie E. Casey Foundation, "Kids Count Data Center," website, 2021. As of July 26, 2021:
https://datacenter.kidscount.org/

Baker, Bryan, *Population Estimates: Illegal Alien Population Residing in the United States: January 2015*, Washington, D.C.: Office of Immigration Statistics, U.S. Department of Homeland Security, December 2018. As of April 2, 2021:
https://www.dhs.gov/sites/default/files/publications/18_1214_PLCY_pops-est-report.pdf

Bojórquez, Kim, "California's Sanctuary Law Upheld by Supreme Court. Here's What It Means," *Sacramento Bee*, June 15, 2020. As of June 28, 2021:
https://www.sacbee.com/news/politics-government/capitol-alert/article243546072.html

Booi, Zenande, Caitlin Callahan, Genevieve Fugere, Mikaela Harris, Alexandra Hughes, Alexander Kramarczuk, Caroline Kurtz, Raimy Reyes, and Sruti Swaminathan, *Ensuring Every Undocumented Student Succeeds: A Report on Access to Public Education for Undocumented Children*, Washington, D.C.: Georgetown Law Human Rights Institute, April 11, 2016. As of April 2, 2021:
https://www.law.georgetown.edu/human-rights-institute/our-work/fact-finding-project/ensuring-every-undocumented-student-succeeds-a-report/

California Department of Education, "Title III FAQs: Immigrant Student Education Program," webpage, last reviewed June 25, 2020a. As of October 7, 2020:
https://www.cde.ca.gov/sp/el/t3/title3faq.asp#Immigrant

———, "English Learner Roadmap," webpage, last reviewed November 3, 2020b. As of April 2, 2021:
https://www.cde.ca.gov/sp/el/rm/index.asp

———, "Bilingual Coordinators Network," webpage, last reviewed January 5, 2021. As of April 2, 2021:
https://www.cde.ca.gov/sp/el/t3/bcn.asp

California Department of Social Services, "California Newcomer Education and Well-Being," webpage, undated. As of April 11, 2021:
https://www.cdss.ca.gov/inforesources/refugees/programs-and-info/youth-initiatives/calnew

Camarota, Steven A., Bryan Griffith, and Karen Zeigler, *Mapping the Impact of Immigration on Public Schools*, Washington, D.C.: Center for Immigration Studies, January 9, 2017. As of April 2, 2021:
https://cis.org/Report/Mapping-Impact-Immigration-Public-Schools

Capps, Randy, Julia Gelatt, Ariel G. Ruiz Soto, and Jennifer Van Hook, *Unauthorized Immigrants in the United States: Stable Numbers, Changing Origins*, Washington, D.C.: Migration Policy Institute, December 2020. As of May 12, 2021:
https://www.migrationpolicy.org/
research/unauthorized-immigrants-united-states-stable-numbers-changing-origins

Cardoza, Kavitha, "How Schools Are Responding to Migrant Children," *Education Week*, April 9, 2019. As of April 2, 2021:
https://www.edweek.org/leadership/how-schools-are-responding-to-migrant-children/2019/04

CBP—*See* U.S. Customs and Border Protection.

Chang-Bacon, Chris K., "Generation Interrupted: Rethinking 'Students with Interrupted Formal Education' (SIFE) in the Wake of a Pandemic," *Educational Researcher*, Vol. 50, No. 3, 2021, pp. 187–196.

Cheatham, Amelia, "Central America's Turbulent Northern Triangle," Council on Foreign Relations, updated July 1, 2021. As of July 23, 2021:
https://www.cfr.org/backgrounder/central-americas-turbulent-northern-triangle

Cherewka, Alexis, "The Digital Divide Hits U.S. Immigrant Households Disproportionately During the COVID-19 Pandemic," Migration Policy Institute, September 3, 2020. As of June 25, 2021:
https://www.migrationpolicy.org/article/
digital-divide-hits-us-immigrant-households-during-covid-19

Chiacu, Doina, "U.S. Facing Biggest Migrant Surge in 20 Years: Homeland Security," Reuters, March 16, 2021. As of April 2, 2021:
https://www.reuters.com/article/us-usa-immigration-border/
u-s-facing-biggest-migrant-surge-in-20-years-homeland-security-idUSKBN2B81M5

Cohn, D'Vera, "How U.S. Immigration Laws and Rules Have Changed Through History," Pew Research Center, September 30, 2015. As of April 2, 2021:
https://www.pewresearch.org/fact-tank/2015/09/30/
how-u-s-immigration-laws-and-rules-have-changed-through-history/

Dee, Thomas, and Mark Murphy, "Vanished Classmates: The Effects of Local Immigration Enforcement on School Enrollment," *American Educational Research Journal*, Vol. 57, No. 2, 2019, pp. 694–727.

DHS—*See* U.S. Department of Homeland Security.

Dickerson, Caitlin, "Parents of 545 Children Separated at the Border Cannot Be Found," *New York Times*, October 21, 2020, updated March 15, 2021. As of April 2, 2021:
https://www.nytimes.com/2020/10/21/us/migrant-children-separated.html

Diffey, Louisa, and Sarah Steffes, *50-State Review: Age Requirements for Free and Compulsory Education*, Denver, Colo.: Education Commission of the States, November 2017.

Dinan, John, "The Institutionalization of State Resistance to Federal Directives in the 21st Century," *The Forum*, Vol. 18, No. 1, 2020, pp. 3–23.

Doan, Sy, David Grant, Daniella Henry, Julia H. Kaufman, Rebecca Ann Lawrence, Andrea Prado Tuma, Claude Messan Setodji, Laura Stelitano, Ashley Woo, and Christopher J. Young, *American Instructional Resources Surveys: 2020 Technical Documentation and Survey Results*, Santa Monica, Calif.: RAND Corporation, RR-A134-4, 2020. As of July 26, 2021: https://www.rand.org/pubs/research_reports/RRA134-4.html

DOJ—*See* U.S. Department of Justice.

ED*Facts* Submission System, *C059—Staff FTE File Specifications*, version 13.1, SY 2016-17, Washington, D.C.: U.S. Department of Education, July 2017. As of April 2, 2021: https://www2.ed.gov/about/inits/ed/edfacts/eden/non-xml/c059-13-1.doc

Enriquez, Laura, "Because We Feel the Pressure and We Also Feel the Support: Examining the Educational Success of Undocumented Immigrant Latina/o Students," *Harvard Educational Review*, Vol. 81, No. 3, 2011, pp. 476–500.

Executive Order 13769, "Protecting the Nation from Foreign Terrorist Entry into the United States," Washington, D.C.: Executive Office of the President, January 27, 2017.

Executive Order 13780, "Protecting the Nation from Foreign Terrorist Entry into the United States," Washington, D.C.: Executive Office of the President, March 6, 2017.

Gelatt, Julia, and Jie Zong, "Settling In: A Profile of the Unauthorized Immigrant Population in the United States," fact sheet, Migration Policy Institute, November 2018. As of April 2, 2021: https://www.migrationpolicy.org/sites/default/files/publications/UnauthorizedData-FactSheet_FinalWeb.pdf

Gonzales, Richard, "Trump's Executive Order on Family Separation: What It Does and Doesn't Do," NPR, June 20, 2018. As of April 2, 2021: https://www.npr.org/2018/06/20/622095441/trump-executive-order-on-family-separation-what-it-does-and-doesnt-do

Gonzales, Roberto G., Carola Suárez-Orozco, and Maria Cecilia Dedios-Sanguineti, "No Place to Belong: Contextualizing Concepts of Mental Health Among Undocumented Immigrant Youth in the United States," *American Behavioral Scientist*, Vol. 57, No. 8, 2013, pp. 1174–1199.

Gonzales, Roberto G., Veronica Terriquez, and Stephen P. Ruszczyk, "Becoming DACAmented: Assessing the Short-Term Benefits of Deferred Action for Childhood Arrivals (DACA)," *American Behavioral Scientist*, Vol. 58, No. 14, October 2014, pp. 1852–1872.

Gramlich, John, "Migrant Apprehensions at U.S.-Mexico Border Are Surging Again," Pew Research Center, March 15, 2021.

Gramlich, John, and Luis Noe-Bustamante, "What's Happening at the U.S.-Mexico Border in 5 Charts," Pew Research Center, November 1, 2019. As of April 2, 2021: https://www.pewresearch.org/fact-tank/2019/11/01/whats-happening-at-the-u-s-mexico-border-in-5-charts/

Hackman, Michelle, "Migrant Arrests at U.S. Southern Border Reach 15-Year High," *Wall Street Journal*, April 2, 2021. As of April 2, 2021: https://www.wsj.com/articles/migrant-arrests-at-u-s-southern-border-reach-15-year-high-11617385246

Hainmueller, Jens, Duncan Lawrence, Linna Martén, Bernard Black, Lucila Figueroa, Michael Hotard, Tomás R. Jiménez, Fernando Mendoza, Maria I. Rodriguez, Jonas J. Swartz, and David D. Laitin, "Protecting Unauthorized Immigrant Mothers Improves Their Children's Mental Health," *Science*, Vol. 357, No. 6355, September 8, 2017, pp. 1041–1044.

Hoefer, Michael, Nancy Francis Rytina, and Bryan Baker, *Estimates of the Unauthorized Immigrant Population Residing in the United States: January 2011*, Washington, D.C.: Office of Immigration Statistics, U.S. Department of Homeland Security, 2012.

Hsin, Amy, and Francesc Ortega, "The Effects of Deferred Action for Childhood Arrivals on the Educational Outcomes of Undocumented Students," *Demography*, Vol. 55, June 2018, pp. 1487–1506.

Immigration Center for Women and Children, "Special Immigrant Juvenile Status," webpage, undated. As of April 2, 2021:
https://www.icwclaw.org/special-immigrant-juvenile-status-sijs

Inchauste, Gabriela, *Poverty and Equity Brief: Mexico*, Washington, D.C.: World Bank Group, April 2020.

International Affairs Office, U.S. Department of Education, "U.S.-Mexico Bilateral Cooperation," December 12, 2015. As of August 17, 2021:
https://www2.ed.gov/about/inits/ed/internationaled/us-mex-bi.html

International Organization for Migration, *World Migration Report 2020*, Geneva, Switzerland, 2019. As of April 19, 2021:
https://publications.iom.int/books/world-migration-report-2020

Jefferson Parish Schools, "Our District and Schools," webpage, undated. As of July 23, 2021:
https://www.jpschools.org/Page/3148

Johnson, Jeh Charles, "Exercising Prosecutorial Discretion with Respect to Individuals Who Came to the United States as Children and with Respect to Certain Individuals Who Are the Parents of U.S. Citizens or Permanent Residents," U.S. Department of Homeland Security, memorandum, November 20, 2014.

Kamarck, Elaine, and Christine Stenglein, "Can Immigration Reform Happen? A Look Back," *FixGov* (blog), Brookings Institution, February 11, 2019a. As of April 2, 2021:
https://www.brookings.edu/blog/fixgov/2019/02/11/can-immigration-reform-happen-a-look-back/

———, "How Many Undocumented Immigrants Are in the United States and Who Are They?" *Voter Vitals* (blog), Brookings Institution, November 12, 2019b. As of April 2, 2021:
https://www.brookings.edu/policy2020/votervital/how-many-undocumented-immigrants-are-in-the-united-states-and-who-are-they/

Kandel, William A., *Unaccompanied Alien Children: An Overview*, Washington, D.C.: Congressional Research Service, R43599, updated October 9, 2019.

———, *The Trump Administration's "Zero Tolerance" Immigration Enforcement Policy*, Washington, D.C.: Congressional Research Service, R45266, updated February 2, 2021. As of April 2, 2021:
https://fas.org/sgp/crs/homesec/R45266.pdf

Kitroeff, Natalie, "2 Hurricanes Devastated Central America: Will the Ruin Spur a Migration Wave?" *New York Times*, December 4, 2020. As of April 2, 2021:
https://www.nytimes.com/2020/12/04/world/americas/guatemala-hurricanes-mudslide-migration.html

Kohut, Andrew, "From the Archives: In '60s, Americans Gave Thumbs-Up to Immigration Law That Changed the Nation," Pew Research Center, September 20, 2019. As of April 2, 2021: https://www.pewresearch.org/fact-tank/2019/09/20/ in-1965-majority-of-americans-favored-immigration-and-nationality-act-2/

Krogstad, Jens Manuel, and Ana Gonzalez-Barrera, "Key Facts About U.S. Immigration Policies and Biden's Proposed Changes," Pew Research Center, March 22, 2021. As of April 2, 2021: https://www.pewresearch.org/fact-tank/2021/03/22/ key-facts-about-u-s-immigration-policies-and-bidens-proposed-changes/

Kuka, Elira, Na'ama Shenhav, and Kevin Shih, "Do Human Capital Decisions Respond to the Returns to Education? Evidence from DACA," *American Economic Journal: Economic Policy*, Vol. 12, No. 1, February 2020, pp. 293–324.

Kwan, Jonathan, "Words Matter: Illegal Immigrant, Undocumented Immigrant, or Unauthorized Immigrant?" Markkula Center for Applied Ethics, Santa Clara University, February 11, 2021. As of April 2, 2021: https://www.scu.edu/ethics/focus-areas/immigration-ethics/immigration-ethics-resources/ immigration-ethics-blog/ words-matter-illegal-immigrant-undocumented-immigrant-or-unauthorized-immigrant/

Lau v. Nichols, 414 U.S. 563, 1974.

Lee, Okhee, "English Language Proficiency Standards Aligned with Content Standards," *Educational Researcher*, Vol. 47, No. 5, 2018, pp. 317–327.

Ligor, Douglas C., *Neither Deportation nor Amnesty: An Alternative for the Immigration Debate Building a Bridge Across the Deportation–Amnesty Divide*, Santa Monica, Calif.: RAND Corporation, PE-279-RC, 2018. As of April 20, 2021: https://www.rand.org/pubs/perspectives/PE279.html

Lhamon, Catherine E., Philip H. Rosenfelt, and Jocelyn Samuels, "Dear Colleague Letter: School Enrollment Procedures," U.S. Department of Justice and U.S. Department of Education, May 8, 2014. As of October 7, 2020: https://www2.ed.gov/about/offices/list/ocr/letters/colleague-201405.pdf

Lustgarten, Abrahm, "The Great Climate Migration," *New York Times Magazine*, July 23, 2020. As of April 2, 2021: https://www.nytimes.com/interactive/2020/07/23/magazine/climate-migration.html

Malakoff, Marguerite, and Kenji Hakuta, "History of Language Minority Education in the United States," in A. M. Padilla, H. H. Fairchild, and C. M. Valadez, eds., *Bilingual Education: Issues and Strategies*, Newbury Park, Calif.: Sage, 1990, pp. 27–43.

Martinez v. Bynum, 461 U.S. 321, 328, 1983.

Marshall, Khiya J., Ximena Urrutia-Rojas, Francisco Soto Mas, and Claudia Coggin, "Health Status and Access to Health Care of Documented and Undocumented Immigrant Latino Women," *Health Care for Women International*, Vol. 26, No. 10, 2005, pp. 916–936.

McDonnell, Lorraine M., and Paul T. Hill, *Newcomers in American Schools: Meeting the Educational Needs of Immigrant Youth*, Santa Monica, Calif.: RAND Corporation, MR-103-AWM/PRIP, 1993. As of April 2, 2021: https://www.rand.org/pubs/monograph_reports/MR103.html

Mendoza, Gilberto Soria, and Noor Shaikh, *Tuition Benefits for Immigrants*, Washington, D.C.: National Conference of State Legislatures, January 16, 2019. As of July 26, 2021: https://www.ncsl.org/research/immigration/tuition-benefits-for-immigrants.aspx

Meyer, Peter J., and Maureen Taft-Morales, *Central American Migration: Root Causes and U.S. Policy*, version 2, Washington, D.C.: Congressional Research Service, IF11151, June 13, 2019.

Migrant Education Program, "State and Regional Contact Information," webpage, undated. As of August 17, 2021:
https://results.ed.gov/resources/coordination_work_group/westpacific/view:list

Migration Policy Institute, "Profile of the Unauthorized Population: United States," webpage, undated. As of April 2, 2021:
https://www.migrationpolicy.org/data/unauthorized-immigrant-population/state/US

―――, *Major U.S. Immigration Laws, 1790–Present*, timeline, Washington, D.C., March 2013. As of April 2, 2021:
https://www.migrationpolicy.org/sites/default/files/publications/CIR-1790Timeline.pdf

Morse, Ann, "Arizona's Immigration Enforcement Laws," National Conference of State Legislatures, revised July 8, 2011. As of May 20, 2021:
https://www.ncsl.org/research/immigration/
analysis-of-arizonas-immigration-law.aspx#Similar_Bills

―――, *Immigrant Policy Project: Report on State Immigration Laws, 2018*, Washington, D.C.: National Conference of State Legislatures, January 2019.

―――, *Immigrant Policy Project: Report on State Immigration Laws, 2019*, Washington, D.C.: National Conference of State Legislatures, March 2020.

―――, *Immigrant Policy Project: Report on State Immigration Laws 2020*, Washington, D.C.: National Conference of State Legislatures, 2021.

Morse, Ann, Maria Pimienta, and Ishanee Chanda, *Report on State Immigration Laws: January–June 2017*, Washington, D.C.: National Conference of State Legislatures, January 2018.

Morse, Ann, Gilberto Soria Mendoza, Connor Jackson, and Joanna Leung, *2016 Report on State Immigration Laws (January–June)*, Washington, D.C.: National Conference of State Legislatures, September 2016.

Napolitano, Janet, "Exercising Prosecutorial Discretion with Respect to Individuals Who Came to the United States as Children," U.S. Department of Homeland Security, memorandum, June 15, 2012.

National Academies of Sciences, Engineering, and Medicine, *Promoting the Educational Success of Children and Youth Learning English: Promising Futures*, Washington, D.C.: National Academies Press, 2017.

National Association of Secondary School Principals, "Undocumented Students," webpage, undated. As of February 26, 2020:
https://www.nassp.org/policy-advocacy-center/nassp-position-statements/
undocumented-students/

National Center for Education Statistics, "American Community Survey—Education Tabulation (ACS-ED)," webpage, Institute of Education Sciences, undated-a. As of April 2, 2021:
https://nces.ed.gov/programs/edge/Demographic/ACS

―――, "Common Core of Data: America's Public Schools," website, Institute of Education Sciences, undated-b. As of April 2, 2021:
https://nces.ed.gov/ccd/

———, "Compulsory School Attendance Laws, Minimum and Maximum Age Limits for Required Free Education, by State: 2017," Table 5.1, Institute of Education Sciences, undated-c. As of April 2, 2021:
https://nces.ed.gov/programs/statereform/tab5_1.asp

———, "ElSi: Elementary/Secondary Information System," web application, Institute of Education Sciences, undated-d. As of April 2, 2021:
https://nces.ed.gov/ccd/elsi/

———, "Percentage of the Population 3 to 34 Years Old Enrolled in School, by Age Group: Selected Years, 1940 Through 2016," Table 103.20, Institute of Education Sciences, January 2018. As of April 2, 2021:
https://nces.ed.gov/programs/digest/d17/tables/dt17_103.20.asp

———, "English Language Learners in Public Schools," webpage, Institute of Education Sciences, last updated May 2020. As of April 2, 2021:
https://nces.ed.gov/programs/coe/indicator_cgf.asp

National Clearinghouse of English Language Acquisition, "Fact Sheets," webpage, undated. As of August 17, 2021:
https://ncela.ed.gov/fact-sheets

NCES—*See* National Center for Education Statistics.

New York State Education Department, "Students with Interrupted/Inconsistent Formal Education (SIFE)," webpage, updated March 12, 2021. As of May 21, 2021:
http://www.nysed.gov/bilingual-ed/students-interruptedinconsistent-formal-education-sife

Ngo, Federick, and Samantha Astudillo, "California DREAM: The Impact of Financial Aid for Undocumented Community College Students," *Educational Researcher*, Vol. 48, No. 1, 2019, pp. 5–18.

Nguyen, Tuan D., Jenna W. Kramer, and Brent J. Evans, "The Effects of Grant Aid on Student Persistence and Degree Attainment: A Systematic Review and Meta-Analysis of the Causal Evidence," *Review of Educational Research*, Vol. 89, No. 6, 2019, pp. 831–874.

Nuñez-Neto, Blas, "Bringing Our Immigration System Back from the Breaking Point," *The Hill*, May 1, 2019. As of April 2, 2021:
https://thehill.com/opinion/immigration/
441556-bringing-the-immigration-system-back-from-the-breaking-point

Oakland Unified School District, "ELL Programs by School and Model," webpage, undated. As of August 17, 2021:
https://www.ousd.org/Page/15146

———, *2018–2021 Roadmap to ELL Achievement*, Oakland, Calif., 2018.

Office of English Language Acquisition, U.S. Department of Education, *English Learner (EL) Trends from the Nation's Report Card*, Washington, D.C., September 2018. As of August 17, 2021:
https://ncela.ed.gov/files/fast_facts/ELs-NAEP_Card.pdf

———, "Fast Sheets," webpage, last updated February 7, 2020. As of August 17, 2021:
https://www2.ed.gov/about/offices/list/oela/fast-facts/index.html

Office of Immigration Statistics, *Efforts by DHS to Estimate Southwest Border Security Between Ports of Entry*, Washington, D.C.: U.S. Department of Homeland Security, September 2017. As of April 2, 2021:
https://www.dhs.gov/sites/default/files/publications/17_0914_estimates-of-border-security.pdf

Office of Refugee Resettlement, "Facts and Data," webpage, last reviewed March 11, 2021. As of April 2, 2021:
https://www.acf.hhs.gov/orr/about/ucs/facts-and-data

ORR—*See* Office of Refugee Resettlement.

Parker, Ben, "Data Shows Scale of Gang Killings in Central America," *New Humanitarian*, February 28, 2020. As of April 2, 2021:
https://www.thenewhumanitarian.org/maps-and-graphics/2020/02/28/
gang-killings-violence-El-Salvador

Passel, Jeffrey S., and D'Vera Cohn, *Unauthorized Immigrant Population: National and State Trends, 2010*, Washington, D.C.: Pew Hispanic Center, Pew Research Center, 2011.

———, *U.S. Unauthorized Immigrant Total Dips to Lowest Level in a Decade*, Washington, D.C.: Pew Research Center, November 27, 2018.

Patler, Caitlin, and Whitney Laster Pirtle, "From Undocumented to Lawfully Present: Do Changes to Legal Status Impact Psychological Wellbeing Among Latino Immigrant Young Adults?" *Social Science and Medicine*, Vol. 199, February 2018, pp. 39–48.

Peck, Sarah Herman, and Ben Harrington, *The "Flores Settlement" and Alien Families Apprehended at the U.S. Border: Frequently Asked Questions*, Washington, D.C.: Congressional Research Service, R45297, updated September 17, 2018.

Pérez, Santiago, and Michelle Hackman, "Migrant Surge at U.S. Border Prompts White House Talks with Mexico, Guatemala," *Wall Street Journal*, March 23, 2021. As of April 2, 2021:
https://www.wsj.com/articles/
senior-u-s-officials-visit-mexico-guatemala-to-address-migrant-surge-11616514413

Pierce, Sarah, *Immigration-Related Policy Changes in the First Two Years of the Trump Administration*, Washington, D.C.: Migration Policy Institute, May 2019. As of April 2, 2021:
https://www.migrationpolicy.org/sites/default/files/publications/
ImmigrationChangesTrumpAdministration-FinalWEB.pdf

Pivovarova, Margarita, and Jeanne Powers, "Are Immigrant Students Disproportionately Consuming Educational Resources?" *Brown Center Chalkboard* (blog), Brookings Institution, October 3, 2019. As of April 2, 2021:
https://www.brookings.edu/blog/brown-center-chalkboard/2019/10/03/
are-immigrant-students-disproportionately-consuming-educational-resources/

Plyler v. Doe, 457 U.S. 202, June 15, 1982.

Public Law 82-414, Immigration and Naturalization Act, June 27, 1952.

Public Law 89-10, Elementary and Secondary Education Act, April 11, 1965.

Public Law 88-352, Civil Rights Act of 1964, July 2, 1964.

Public Law 101-649, Immigration Act of 1990, November 29, 1990.

Public Law 104-193, The Personal Responsibility and Work Opportunity Reconciliation Act of 1996, August 22, 1996.

Public Law 104-208, Omnibus Consolidated Appropriations Act, September 30, 1996.

Public Law 114-95, Every Student Succeeds Act; Title IV, 21st Century Schools; Part A, Student Support and Academic Enrichment Grants, December 10, 2015.

Public Law 107-173, Enhanced Border Security and Visa Entry Reform Act, May 14, 2002.

Public Law 107-296, Homeland Security Act of 2002, November 25, 2002.

Public Law 109-367, Secure Fence Act of 2006, October 26, 2006.

Public Law 116-136, Coronavirus Aid, Relief, and Economic Security Act, March 27, 2020.

Reno v. Flores, 507 U.S. 292, 1993.

Rose, Joel, "Immigration Agencies Ordered Not to Use Term 'Illegal Alien' Under New Biden Policy," NPR, April 19, 2021. As of April 21, 2021:
https://www.npr.org/2021/04/19/988789487/
immigration-agencies-ordered-not-to-use-term-illegal-alien-under-new-biden-polic

Rosenblum, Marc R., and Hongwei Zhang, *Fiscal Year 2020 Enforcement Lifecycle Report*, Washington, D.C.: Office of Immigration Statistics, U.S. Department of Homeland Security, December 2020. As of April 2, 2021:
https://www.dhs.gov/sites/default/files/publications/immigration-statistics/Special_Reports/
Enforcement_Lifecycle/2020_enforcement_lifecycle_report.pdf

Serna, Gabriel R., Joshua M. Cohen, and David H. K. Nguyen, "State and Institutional Policies on In-State Resident Tuition and Financial Aid for Undocumented Students: Examining Constraints and Opportunities," *Education Policy Analysis Archives*, Vol. 25, No. 18, February 27, 2017.

Singer, Audrey, and William A. Kandal, *Immigration: Recent Apprehension Trends at the U.S. Southwest Border*, Washington, D.C.: Congressional Research Service, R46012, November 19, 2019.

Smith, Hillel R., *Expedited Removal of Aliens: Legal Framework*, Washington, D.C.: Congressional Research Service, R45314, updated October 8, 2019.

Southern Poverty Law Center, "Family Separation Under the Trump Administration—a Timeline," webpage, June 17, 2020. As of April 2, 2021:
https://www.splcenter.org/news/2020/06/17/
family-separation-under-trump-administration-timeline

State of Louisiana, *Louisiana Medicaid Eligibility Manual*, Baton Rouge, La., February 26, 2021. As of June 28, 2021:
https://ldh.la.gov/assets/medicaid/MedicaidEligibilityPolicy/I-300.PDF

Suro, Roberto, and Hannah Findling, "State and Local Aid for Immigrants During the COVID-19 Pandemic: Innovating Inclusion," Sol Price Center for Social Innovation, University of Southern California, July 8, 2020.

Sussis, Matthew, *The History of the* Flores *Settlement: How a 1997 Agreement Cracked Open Our Detention Laws*, Washington, D.C.: Center for Immigration Studies, February 11, 2019. As of October 7, 2020:
https://cis.org/Report/History-Flores-Settlement

Takemoto, Tyler, "Understanding the Causes of Migration from Central America," *Pacific Council Magazine*, January 22, 2019. As of April 2, 2021:
https://www.pacificcouncil.org/newsroom/understanding-causes-migration-central-america

Thornley, Alyssa, "ESSA Basics: What Are Title I and Title III?" *TransACT Blog*, May 24, 2017. As of October 7, 2020:
https://www.transact.com/blog/essa-basics-what-are-title-i-and-title-iii

TRAC Reports, "Border Patrol Arrests," webpage, undated-a. As of April 2, 2021:
https://trac.syr.edu/phptools/immigration/cbparrest/

———, "Juveniles—Immigration Court Deportation Proceedings," webpage, undated-b. As of April 2, 2021:
https://trac.syr.edu/phptools/immigration/juvenile/

UNICEF—*See* United Nations Children's Fund.

United Nations Children's Fund, *Central America: Hurricanes Eta and Iota*, Humanitarian Situation Report No. 7, New York, January 15, 2021. As of April 2, 2021:
https://www.unicef.org/media/91211/file/Central-America-Humanitarian-SitRep-Hurricanes-ETA-and-Iota-15%20January-2021.pdf

United Nations Economic Commission for Latin America and the Caribbean, "Femicide or Feminicide," webpage, undated. As of April 2, 2021:
https://oig.cepal.org/en/indicators/femicide-or-feminicide

United Nations High Commissioner for Refugees, *Why "Undocumented" or "Irregular"?* leaflet, Geneva, Switzerland, September 2018. As of April 2, 2021:
https://www.unhcr.org/cy/wp-content/uploads/sites/41/2018/09/TerminologyLeaflet_EN_PICUM.pdf

United States Code, Title 8, Aliens and Nationality; Chapter 12, Immigration and Nationality; Subchapter II, Immigration; Part IV, Inspection, Apprehension, Examination, Exclusion, and Removal; Section 1232, Enhancing Efforts to Combat the Trafficking of Children.

United States Code, Title 42, The Public Health and Welfare; Chapter 6a, Public Health Service.

U.S. Citizenship and Immigration Services, *Welcome to the United States: A Guide for New Immigrants*, Washington, D.C., 2015.

U.S. Customs and Border Protection, "Southwest Land Border Encounters," webpage, last modified April 9, 2021. As of April 20, 2021:
https://www.cbp.gov/newsroom/stats/sw-border-migration

U.S. Department of Education, *Fact Sheet I: Educational Services for Immigrant Children and Those Recently Arrived to the United States*, Washington, D.C., September 19, 2014a. As of April 2, 2021:
https://www2.ed.gov/policy/rights/guid/unaccompanied-children.html

———, *Fact Sheet II: Additional Questions and Answers on Enrolling New Immigrant Students*, Washington, D.C., December 2014b. As of April 2, 2021:
https://www2.ed.gov/policy/rights/guid/unaccompanied-children-2.pdf

———, "Key Policy Letters Signed by the Education Secretary or Deputy Secretary," webpage, last modified, March 2, 2017a. As of October 7, 2020:
https://www2.ed.gov/policy/elsec/guid/secletter/151019.html

———, "Educational Resources for Immigrants, Refugees, Asylees, and Other New Americans," webpage, last modified September 5, 2017b. As of October 7, 2020:
https://www2.ed.gov/about/overview/focus/immigration-resources.html

U.S. Department of Health, Education and Welfare, *Task Force Findings Specifying Remedies Available for Eliminating Past Educational Practices Ruled Unlawful Under* Lau v. Nichols, Washington, D.C., August 1975.

U.S. Department of Homeland Security, "Migrant Protection Protocols," webpage, January 24, 2019a. As of April 2, 2021:
https://www.dhs.gov/news/2019/01/24/migrant-protection-protocols

———, *Department of Homeland Security Border Security Metrics Report*, Washington, D.C., February 26, 2019b. As of April 2, 2021:
https://www.dhs.gov/sites/default/files/publications/
ndaa_border_metrics_report_fy_2018_0_0.pdf

———, "Inadmissibility on Public Charge Grounds," *Federal Register*, Vol. 84, No. 157, August 14, 2019c.

———, "DHS Announces Process to Address Individuals in Mexico with Active MPP Cases," press release, February 11, 2021. As of April 2, 2021:
https://www.dhs.gov/news/2021/02/11/
dhs-announces-process-address-individuals-mexico-active-mpp-cases

U.S. Department of Justice, "Title VI of the Civil Rights Act of 1964," webpage, undated. As of April 2, 2021:
https://www.justice.gov/crt/fcs/TitleVI

———, "Enforcement of Title VI of the Civil Rights Act of 1964—National Origin Discrimination Against Persons with Limited English Proficiency; Policy Guidance," *Federal Register*, Vol. 65, No. 159, August 16, 2000, pp. 50123–50125.

U.S. Government Accountability Office, *Southwest Border: Actions Needed to Improve DHS Processing of Families and Coordination Between DHS and HHS*, Washington, D.C., GAO-20-245, February 2020. As of July 27, 2021:
https://www.gao.gov/products/gao-20-245

Vaughan, Jessica M., and Bryan Griffith, "Map: Sanctuary Cities, Counties, and States," Center for Immigration Studies, updated March 22, 2021. As of March 22, 2021:
https://cis.org/Map-Sanctuary-Cities-Counties-and-States

Villalobos, José Ángel Córdorva, and Arne Duncan, "Annex IX to the Memorandum of Understanding on Education Between the Government of the United Mexican States and the Government of the United States of America," Secretariat of Public Education of the United Mexican states and U.S. Department of Education, November 2018. As of August 17, 2021:
https://www2.ed.gov/admins/tchrqual/learn/signedannexixtomoueng.pdf

Warren, Robert, "US Undocumented Population Continued to Fall from 2016 to 2017, and Visa Overstays Significantly Exceeded Illegal Crossings for the Seventh Consecutive Year," New York: Center for Migration Studies, 2017. As of April 2, 2021:
https://cmsny.org/publications/essay-2017-undocumented-and-overstays/

———, "In 2019, the US Undocumented Population Continued a Decade-Long Decline and the Foreign-Born Population Neared Zero Growth," *Journal on Migration and Human Security*, March 2021.

Washington Office of Superintendent of Public Instruction, *Immigrant Student Identification: Definitions and Procedures*, Olympia, revised October 2017. As of October 7, 2020:
https://www.k12.wa.us/sites/default/files/public/migrantbilingual/pubdocs/
tbipguidelinesimmigrant.pdf

Watson, Julie, "Biden Lifts Trump-Era Ban Blocking Legal Immigration to U.S.," Associated Press, February 25, 2021. As of May 16, 2021:
https://apnews.com/article/joe-biden-donald-trump-coronavirus-pandemic-immigration-united-states-3f87c625b476161feb8e6c77256e2597

Weiss, Jane Charlotte, and Martha Garrett Sandstead, "English Learners and English Language Arts Education," English Learners Success Forum, undated. As of May 16, 2021:
https://www.elsuccessforum.org/
resources/english-learners-and-english-language-arts-education

Williams, Erica, Eric Figueroa, and Wesley Tharpe, *Inclusive Approach to Immigrants Who Are Undocumented Can Help Families and States Prosper*, Washington, D.C.: Center on Budget and Policy Priorities, December 19, 2019. As of April 2, 2021:
https://www.cbpp.org/research/state-budget-and-tax/
inclusive-approach-to-immigrants-who-are-undocumented-can-help

Wong, Tom K., Gabriel De Roche, and Jesus Rojas Venzor, "The Migrant 'Surge' at the U.S. Southern Border Is Actually a Predictable Pattern," *Washington Post*, March 25, 2021. As of April 2, 2021:
https://www.washingtonpost.com/politics/2021/03/23/
theres-no-migrant-surge-us-southern-border-heres-data/

World Bank, "The World Bank in Guatemala," webpage, undated-a. As of September 1, 2021:
https://www.worldbank.org/en/country/guatemala/overview

———, "The World Bank in Honduras," webpage, undated-b. As of September 1, 2021:
https://www.worldbank.org/en/country/honduras

About the Authors

Shelly Culbertson is a senior policy researcher at the RAND Corporation. Her research focuses on education, mass migration, disaster recovery, and international development. She has an M.P.A. in public policy and international development.

Julia H. Kaufman is a senior policy researcher at the RAND Corporation. Her research focuses on how states and school systems can support high-quality instruction and student learning, as well as methods for measuring educator perceptions and instruction. She has a Ph.D. in international education.

Jenna W. Kramer is an associate policy researcher at the RAND Corporation. Her work uses quasi-experimental, experimental, and qualitative designs to examine human capital development decisions and transitions, particularly for students at community and technical colleges. She has a Ph.D. in education policy.

Brian Phillips is a senior quantitative analyst at the RAND Corporation. Themes of his work include educational program evaluation, workforce development and management, economic impact analysis, infrastructure planning and financing, and health care costs and utilization. He has an M.P.A. in economics and public policy.